Multidimensional Living:

Moving Beyond Astral Adventures

Sharon Ann Meyer

This book is dedicated to humanity as we collectively move up the spiral of evolution to once again become multidimensional beings in form and formless states.

Contents

PART TWO:

Dreams

PART THREE:

Departed Loved Ones Speak

PART FOUR:

Multidimensional Living

Preface

Unfolding the god-given gifts of clairvoyance and intuition, which every human is born with, has assisted me in seeing, sometimes hearing, and knowing without physical evidence more than the usual five senses allow. Throughout these past few years I've continually received guidance, from more evolved aspects of my very own consciousness (which is all any of us receive) that often gets forgotten upon living in the moment of Now. And so, publication of this book is possible because I've learned to document messages and occurrences that are still available to me, miraculously, despite numerous location moves and losing multiple computer hard drives. In addition to hosting some of the guidance received, this book offers selected examples of experiences beyond the usual limited 3D-4D frequencies.

For those experiencing unprecedented struggle and strife, have faith things will improve, if you allow them to, by tapping into your own god-given gifts of clairvoyance and intuition. Private thoughts within my 2008 journal note just how far I have come in this journey of experience and expression:

"The only thing that gets me through the days and nights is the knowledge that this world is a dream. I am so very lucky to have so many constant reminders of the illusory world we seem to live in. I think I would have found a way to kill this body if it was not for the spirit of my last born son."

Hence, my state of mind while moving through yet another "dark night of the soul," and yes, those dark nights are numerous.

Thank you to all those who have gone before me to guide and console, quotes such as the following from Joseph Campbell in *Reflections on the Art of Living* helped:

"The dark night of the soul

comes just before revelation.

When everything is lost,

and all seems darkness,

then comes the new life

and all that is needed."

Addendum: HU-man Potential

Potentials for humans are, as unbelievable as it may sound, unlimited. We live in a field of oscillating frequency, ever-changing and ready to accept us into its frequency upon our belief and conscious effort. In addition to the physical body, we also have several bodies, which many metaphysicians tap into at will. In what might be referred to as layers, beyond the physical frame frequency a higher frequency known as the etheric body exists, and beyond this lays the astral body. There are more layers to our very BEingness, such as the Mental/Causual body but for the purpose of this book, we shall limit our discussion to the first three bodies now available to many more humans than ever before, as each opens up to the frequencies and evolutionary possibilities.

When we sleep, we move beyond the physical and then etheric body to the astral frequency where, as with each frequency, many frequencies/realms/layers exist. The astral realm frequency in which we normally tap into is the one in which we relate to the most with our own body frequency during waking hours. This is not to say that we don't have the ability, nor in fact tap into higher frequencies, but merely to point out the importance of maintaining the highest frequency possible during waking hours, by concentrating only on those things we wish to see in our world.

Everyone has the ability to tap into a wide variety of frequencies, and many times do unknowingly, for instance, during sleep and meditation. Each emotion, thought, word, reaction or deed changes our body's frequency because we live in a participatory universe of our very own making. Now, as one remains in the waking state one also has the ability to tap into the astral and mental realms. Recognizing when these times occur and moving through them consciously can enrich our experience while in human form.

Enjoy the astral adventure accounts and higher frequency experiences from this illusion, which are titled for easy reference. Chapter material is categorized chronologically so one can see how increasing sixth sense consciousness occurred for the author. May this information assist you while evolving into the multidimensional HU-man we are all meant to experience and express!

PART ONE

Beginning Astral
Frequency Adventures

Early Explorations

When I first began to connect with the astral world I was totally unaware of what was happening, what it meant, or that after a short period of agreeing to assist departed souls with their unfinished business, it would evolve to the point where I decided to leave this ability behind to tap into higher frequencies, quite a step up from not even knowing there are multiple frequencies in which we humans may experience and express—physical, astral, mental and causal.

Whether you choose to experience the astral realm, or not, is your personal choice. As Robert Monroe notes in his book *Far Journeys* the end point of the game we're in is set, but we can use our free will to change how and when we get there. It's what we do, between the time when our consciousness enters earth and leaves earth that's a part of the game. So, consider using your free will wisely to experience and express in ever expanding unique ways!

Departed Loved Ones Unfinished Business

This excerpt from my first book, *THE END OF MY SOAP OPERA LIFE :-) DEATH OF THE SUN,* relates some of the first communications from my departed son, feelings upon receiving them and reactions of family members, to assist those who may experience similar circumstances.

County medical examiners autopsy Daniel's body because his death is an accident. The body is ready for viewing at the funeral home three days later. But Samantha refuses to go. Sedated by painkillers, she seems possessed.

Samantha works constantly, while in the Lazy Boy, where sleep overwhelmed her on the fateful night of Daniel's death. In her mind, his soul remains in the middle, trying to clean the mess seemingly left behind. There's a task to do in a hurry, and as Samantha reviews family videos, she must find bits and pieces of Daniel for a new video. This video must feature him happy, joking, as he did many, many, times. It's a difficult task but she's up to the challenge. Everyone thinks she's still in shock, while refusing to view his body or attend the funeral.

"She's in denial, still in shock," many of them say. "Just leave her alone to deal with it."

Samantha knows she's doing exactly what Daniel wants as she continues with the videos. There are at least thirty videotapes, six hours each, to edit. Daniel's soul remains to

3

guide her through the process. Feeling fortunate to have bought a double VCR player/recorder right before his physical death, she hasn't yet learned there are no coincidences. The purchase made the plan work.

Family members note she needs the closure of seeing Daniel's dead body. They demand that she eventually "faces reality" to admit he's gone.

Samantha sleeps in the chair for a number of days. As when physically alive, Daniel still telepathically communicates. Samantha hears him clearly. Although no audible words are spoken, his thoughts flow freely from the Otherside as she sits in the dark living room, with closed blinds. She doesn't share this information knowing that everyone will call her crazy.

Rachel schedules Daniel's funeral for the day after the viewing at the church where they married. Samantha still feels driven to work on the videotape, even when Esther comes to console her from Michigan. A great, unexplainable urge to finish the video consumes her.

"You've been through enough Mom," Samantha hears Daniel say each time anyone asks her to attend the funeral. "You don't need to go to the dog and pony show."

Everyone looks at her as if she's crazy when she says Daniel does not want her at the funeral.

Friends visit to offer condolences and deliver food before continuing on to the funeral. Rebecca's friend since high school, Lydia, her husband Joseph, and mother Hannah, arrives to set up tables in the back yard for the wake. Samantha hasn't met Joseph or Hannah who has brain cancer and wears a red bandana upon her shaved head. Their helpfulness soon overwhelms her.

The trio sets up chairs and tables, and puts food on kitchen counters, as Samantha continues to work. Later in the day, Hannah talks with Samantha of her recent move to Lydia and Joseph's house and ongoing cancer treatments. She writes a lovely poem for Abigail about Daddy Daniel in Heaven. Hannah ends the poem with "Amen." Lydia announces that all of Hannah's poems end the same special way.

Daniel's soul doesn't want sorrow but knows people have to deal with physical death. Few people attend the wake compared to those who attend the funeral. Some of Daniel's closest friends choose not to come. Samantha isn't sure why, but really doesn't care, as Daniel's soul directs her to distribute videotapes, for interested friends and family.

Samantha remains busy making copies of the master videotape. The finished video makes it easy to see who Daniel really was. It covers his life from age seventeen to thirty-six years of age. There isn't much more to add since the family saw him increasingly less during his last year of life. She has not even considered visiting with Daniel's wife and daughter since the accident. When they arrive with the rest of their family, she's happy but feeling a bit guilty. Samantha finally leaves her task when people move out to the back yard.

A strong gust of air blows past as she opens the back screen door. Daniel's unmistakable presence flows joyously in the wind. He's happy to be free. The feeling is undeniable. Samantha's knees weaken and she nearly drops to the ground.

"I'm free Mom," Daniel shouts inside her brain. "I'm free!"

Her heart fills with joy even as tears flow down fat, red cheeks. But she doesn't tell anyone fearing that they'll think her crazy. It's the first of many times that she feels his presence so strongly.

Bomb Scare

As the veils between worlds, frequencies if you will, continue to oscillate and merge, allowing us to become more in tune with numerous frequencies at a time, we may not always be aware of developing psychic abilities as noted with this event, which is documented in my second book, *THE END OF MY SOAP OPERA LIFE :-) A Change In Perception*:

New words fill my mind upon waking on Christmas Eve. We canceled newspaper delivery, to save money, and I have not watched television news for many months so there's no reasonable explanation for the message.

"There was a bomb threat earlier today."

Two days later, while cleaning a cluttered table in the living room, I find a section of newspaper dated December 24, 2005 that James brought home from work. A headline reports, "Bomb Scare Closes I-95, Guns Found." My psychic abilities are rising.

Family Message

The first astral message received from someone I barely knew, the mother of my daughter's friend, was totally unexpected.

"Hannah is back in the hospital, for the last time. She makes her transition on July 15, 2005. I learn about it in an unusual way, two days later, while repeating blessings at 3:00 AM. A clear flow of odd words effortlessly enters my head after saying the usual prayer. I quickly associate them with Hannah.

"Hannah passed slowly, into the light, ready to start life anew. Everyone watched her, as she slowly went, waiting to greet her with love."

"Wait, wait," I think excitedly, "am I supposed to remember these words?"

The words continue. If I'm to remember them, I will.

"No one was noisy. No one was loud. They respected her wisdom and knew. Do not be saddened. Don't be afraid. Always be open. Fill your heart with love and know she is happy again. Amen. May God fill your heart with Light and Love."

The key word for me is Amen. Hannah used that word to end a poem she wrote for Abigail about her daddy the year before. Clearly, these words are for Hannah's children. I am to be the messenger. The words repeat in my head as I quickly make my way into the office to get a pen and paper. I write them down,

8

knowing there will be an opportunity to give them to their intended recipients.

In the morning, I watch the video of our trip to Florida's west coast and decide to make a slide show of Hannah. It takes several hours to extract pictures from the video and set them to music. I plan on giving the video and Hannah's message to her children.

Rebecca telephones two days later to tell me Hannah passed away, in the middle of the night, alone in her hospital bed. We attend Hannah's memorial together but she's skeptical when I tell her about the message.

"I don't think this is the time for your nonsense Mother," she states with a smirk.

I'm determined to deliver the message. The opportunity arises when we go to Lydia's home after the service. Everyone is surprised to see the slide show play on Lydia's DVD player as I quickly turn to Hannah's children.

"Your mother," I say excitedly looking from Lydia to her brother, "wanted you to know she didn't suffer. She wants you to know she is happy on the Otherside."

Their stares portray disbelief and apprehension as they ponder how to react. It's clear they do not believe 'Crazy Nana'.

"It doesn't matter to me what you think for my job is done," I announce, handing them copies of the message, before walking to the patio in search of my drink."

Astral Vision

𝕿he following is an excerpt from my second book, *THE END OF MY SOAP OPERA LIFE :-) A Change In Perception.*

Morning messages continue, such as, "Go forth with a blessing upon your heart for you are free". One morning while experiencing gross spine and joint pain, I ask for relief and wonder why I have not seen the indigo blue lights mentioned by departed Annie in the language of the lights (dyingtoliveagain.com). I tell myself they are there and see them promptly with eyes closed, two floating like amoeba blobs. What is spirit communicating to me? The image of an ant walking across a bed sheet unfolds behind closed eyes; it's in the upper left field of my vision.

"Why am I seeing such a thing?"

Noting that words in my head could be those of my ego, I ask for an image to see behind closed eyes, and then, less confused, realize the ant had been an image. Almost unbearable, but familiar, heat envelopes my chest area. The mind/body pain still feels intense so I think of joyful things and laugh, before saying a prayer of thanks to God and asking for words to carry me through the day.

"All things pass sayeth the Lord," I hear.

I thank Jesus for being the Voice of God and giving the words to me, start to rise, open my eyes and look to the left. In the upper left of my field of vision lays a small brown ant! After thanking the motionless ant for coming I bless and carry it in my hands, put it on the counter and forget about it.

Heightened Vision

As noted in this excerpt from my third book, *Lightworker's Log: Transformation*, we can experience greatly enhanced vision when our frequency rises.

The next morning, I reaffirm my belief in the exquisite wonder of the sun, noticing floating dust upon waking to the brilliance of golden yellow sunlight streaming in through the east windows. Hair brushes over my face as I rise to a sitting position, and again, witness the real beauty of creation. Specks of twinkling star-shaped white matter float down pass my vision, throughout a cloud of dust. Twirling pieces of substance make their way effortlessly through the floating Stuff of Matter as I gaze filled with wonder.

Brown strings of hair turn into striated strands of see-through taffy while I stare. Each piece holds multiple circles of rainbow colors, particularly noticeable where the strands of hair bend. I look in wonder for several minutes remembering an earlier instance of seeing my hair like this. The rainbow circles scatter haphazardly with some on top of others while other circles line up next to each other. It seems impossible for me to try to duplicate the way it appears.

After a few minutes, I begin to move my fingers slowly to experiment with the strands of hair. Each hair seems to have at least thirty bands of substance running through it lengthwise. I suspect the strands are far more than what I can see even with what appears to be my current, greatly heightened, sense of vision.

I try to remove the rainbow colored orbs by sliding my fingers through the hair but the orbs remain. The very substance of the universe drifts past strands of hair as I look at them in great astonishment. Of course, I've seen the substance and matter of the universe many times but still am amazed that YES; we live in a gigantic bowl of soup!

Two digital pictures of my hair do not reveal the majesty I see. There's no doubt I'll continue to try and document the wonders of the sun as I open a software program on the laptop to try.

Invisible Entities

January 2007 brought my first what I referred to as a negative entity experience. *Manifesting: Lightworker's Log*, my fourth book, documents this event.

Talking to Heaven, a book in which author James Van Praagh writes of departed souls needing help with unfinished business, then occupies the night. It reminds me of how both Daniel and Hannah easily came through me, from the other side, to help with their unfinished business. I now silently agree to continue helping newly departed beings through greater awareness. But I fail to clarify exactly when, and who, can channel through me.

Before drifting off to sleep, after eleven o'clock in the evening, I think about verbalizing my usual welcome to Higher Beings for help, protection, guidance, etc. But I'm too tired. Something unexpected happens right before midnight.

An invisible presence enters the room when I'm on the verge of deep sleep. It feels human. I sense it but am very tired and do not want to open my eyes. The image of a dark, looming figure now appears closer, next to my left side. Even though communication with this presence is possible, between this state of sleep and wakefulness, I do not acknowledge it. As I continue to ignore it, there's a pressing weight upon me, as if; it's trying to enter my body.

Panic rises when the pressure increases as if something is laying on me.

By now, I'm somewhat awake and trying to say something, only the words come out garbled. I'm not mumbling but trying to shout or speak rather loudly. After about thirty seconds, I say something like "Stop it. I do not want you here if you are not a Higher Being."

The presence is gone in an instant. Out of the corner of my right eye, the twinkle of a light appears. It's a strong light, larger than the ones usually seen throughout the day. The battery light on the laptop, sitting on the floor to my left, flickers, as it does when the screen goes black, so I open the laptop up. Sure enough, the computer screen is black again. I leave it on thinking that perhaps the spirit will release it in the morning.

◆

Also documented within the pages of *Manifesting: Lightworker's Log* is another 2007 experience at an unpleasant downtown Tampa, Florida hotel:

Two hours later, while lying on the bed with closed eyes listening to my daily CD, I again feel a spirit. It hovers slightly above me and feels like the same one that visited last night. This time it seems somewhat harmful and tries to hold me down. I cannot move my arms. I bless it and announce that I'm the Light of God and only the Light of God can come near me.

"God, the Living Spirit Almighty, is within me," I silently announce. "I AM the Light of God and only good, and Light, and Love can come near me."

I still cannot move my arms or hands so I repeat the words. Each time I say them, my hands become freer and freer until I finally push them out spread-eagle to both sides of the bed. And then, I open my eyes to look around the room. Nothing is there. My eyes close again while repeating the usual blessing for all spirits passing or that have passed in the area. I give them everything they need to pass into the Light, lovingly, peacefully, joyfully, astutely, and wholly.

At the beginning of 2008, when house and cat sitting for a friend, I had another 4D experience that did not involve my departed son. Enjoying the wonderful opportunity to rest and reconnect with my spiritual Self, dreams consistently reminded me of the power of God within, and my ability to use it. Departed loved ones continued to offer messages of hope and warnings of things to come as I moved through the arduous process of a third much needed, but unwanted, divorce. Bravely facing an uncertain future, it was time to realize that there is no past, nor future; there is only Now.

And within that Now is everything. During this time I studied *A Course in Miracles* and listened to *His* Words, vowing to continue with *His* work, always recognizing when alone time was needed to clear my space from the vast illusions of earth life. Fleeting holy instants confirmed there is more than I could physically see. Increased awareness of the One in which we live, and move, and have our being made words like consciousness and 'levels' merely ways to point out differences, and yet, the awareness of Oneness continued to light my cumbersome path, while blessing all living things with ever-increasing awareness of the One in which we live, and move, and have all BEing. Strong faith in my ability to withstand any drama trying to penetrate increased awareness of the Truth continued, yet, swaying as palm trees during hurricanes.

Weird things continued to occur while at my friend's sanctuary, even after I used past-life Shaman powers to clear the house, knowing her beloved husband's lingering illness and subsequent death there—by self-imposed starvation—affected its frequency. One day, while sitting in the comfy brown lounger with the old, blind cat on my lap, reading *The Power of Now*, CDs played in the background. Just as hours before Daniel made his 2004 transition, I felt suddenly tired and instantly fell asleep (in a nutshell: this is another sign of changing frequencies while 'waking up' to multiple states of awareness). But I woke less than an hour later, still feeling an uncontrollable urge to sleep, so I closed my eyes again surprised to hear beautiful music, birds singing, ocean waves, and meditation music. As I listened I heard whales and knew it was CD number 95.

As soon as I recognized the CD a very strong vibrational field enveloped me. Not sure whether awake or asleep, there was an increase in my own body's rate of vibration, unmatched by anything felt to date. It seemed as if my body was shaking uncontrollably, as if very cold, and then there came a sense of something else in the room. At first I thought it was my friend returning early and silently asked if she wanted to rest on the lounger as I offered to get up. And then, I seemed to feel apprehensive, not threatened exactly, but unsure of what was going on. My mind then drew on the power of God and I heard myself say "I AM the Light of God." And with a smug satisfaction, "Nothing can harm the Light of God." I then recognized that I might seem a bit egotistic and that if I was being fearful it not only fed any negativity but was not conductive to doing what I should be doing, which is sending love.

And so with the great vibration still soaring through my body I again said, "I AM the Light of God," and then told the entity it was so loved as I mentally hugged it full of the sense of love. At that moment, the uncertainness seemed to disappear and my rate of vibration decreased slightly. I could hear Amber purring loudly on my lap and thought to bless any entity in the area that might be passing to the Otherside.

After silently repeating the usual blessing, I opened my eyes to look about the room. Nothing in the room was different. Although it was a bit chilly, for me, at 72-degrees Fahrenheit, wearing just an undershirt and lounging pants, I was not cold. As the much younger cat watched curiously from the lounger chair next to us, yet remained unmoving, so unlike the troublesome rascal, I closed my eyes again for a few minutes to contemplate what had just occurred. Joy filled me upon knowing my awareness is beginning to change, yet again, in a good way, as part of the process of evolving spiritual awareness.

Sending Cassadaga Spirits Into The Light

On Thursday the seventh of January 2008, I leave with my younger sister Ruth to drive our youngest sister Sarah home after a weeks visit in Fort Lauderdale. The drive to Sarah's house, near Tampa about four hours away, is somewhat exciting as my CD player keeps stopping and starting. Sarah and I give one another knowing looks for we know Daniel, my departed son's energy, is with us. Certain key words and songs sporadically repeat as we drive along the freeway. We almost give up listening to the music and at times just talk as the CD plays but seems to pause for several minutes; for even though the display says "play," nothing is heard.

Ruth and I plan to spend the night at a hotel because she has tomorrow off from work so there's no great need to drive right back to Fort Lauderdale after dropping Sarah off. Ruth had wanted to stay at a hotel further down the road, but, days ago, for some unknown reason, I reserved one that was only about thirty minutes from Sarah's house. So now we drop Sarah off and head back towards home to stay at a Marriott Residence Inn for the night, reserved with my daughter's employee discount. As we drive, Ruth talks of a spooky place she heard about called Cassadaga (http://www.cassadagahotel.net/). I remember it as a place where psychic mediums live and work.

"Well, I've heard about Cassadaga and I've always wanted to go there," Ruth notes excitedly. "I think it's around here."

"You know," I reply, turning to look at her while sensing our adventure will expand, "it must be nearby because my friend Mary who lives an hour further away from here goes there frequently for readings."

Now smiling widely, Ruth suddenly becomes excited at the thought of actually going there. "Well, gee, I wonder if I can get Naomi to work for me. I've got tomorrow off but have to be in early on Saturday. I wonder if she would cover for me so I could actually have two days off in a row."

"Why don't you call her and ask?" I reply adamantly, while a part of me thinks, "Oh, dear, I only packed for one night."

Of course, in line with events that are meant to occur, Naomi quickly agrees to work for Ruth, in my mind a small miracle! Ruth's excitement now visibly increases at the thought of an unplanned adventure, while intuition tells me the trip is important. I really have no desire to go to Cassadaga but recognize we are guided to do so. Is it solely for Ruth's benefit? Nevertheless, too many years have passed us by without the uninterrupted pleasure of each other's company so I look forward to the time.

Shortly after checking into the Residence Inn for the night, my knowledgeable friend Mary answers questions as to who to see for the best reading. Since Ruth frequently stays at hotels for her job, she knows the Inn offers computers for guest use. After dinner at a nice restaurant, plans for the next two days fall into place as we use the sparsely booked hotel's computer; and much to my dismay, after getting directions to Cassadaga, Ruth voices a strong preference to stay at the haunted 100-year old hotel. As someone who senses unseen energies very strongly, this is the last thing I want to do, but quelling the desire to voice this I remain silent as we make the reservations before returning to our comfy suite.

At ten o'clock in the morning and with open car windows amid perfect weather we begin our ninety-minute drive to Cassadaga.

A surreal scene greets us upon entering the very small town featuring our next reserved stay. As we walk through another nearly empty hotel, this one with a strange and gloomy atmosphere, filled with dark wood, I again sense our stay will be significant. Upon questioning a lone visitor we learn it is going to be very, very cold at night. Unlike our usually mild Florida winter hours away in Fort Lauderdale, area freeze warnings have everyone expecting it to be 32 degrees by morning! Some people even expect snow! I had no conscious idea of the impending bitter weather while packing, but amazingly intuition led me to bring a pair of warm pants, socks, wristbands, a warm stocking hat and cotton gloves. Yes! My Higher Self always knows what is going on, even if I don't, so I'm ever grateful to follow the prompts that lead me to do things I would not normally do.

Unlike most hotels where the check-in desk is clearly apparent, it takes more time for us to find the woman who took our telephone reservation. She sits behind a very old, small wooden desk in the gift shop, and soon verifies that it will to be very cold tonight. Since we reserved one of the cheaper, upper rooms at $70 per night, and they are poorly heated, the room will not be as warm and cozy as ones on the first floor.

"I'm prepared to make you a deal," she announces with a wide grin. Ruth perks up and asks to be in a room with a lot of ghosts as I look on in horror.

"Well then," says the knowing woman with a now toothy smile, "I am prepared to offer you the best room that we have, the largest suite that we have, which usually costs $130 a night, for only ninety dollars. It is only twenty dollars more than what you have prepared to pay."

Could this be a sign? Are we to stay in the large suite? Why stay in one small room and be cold when we can stay in a luxurious two-room suite with a bathroom on the warm, cozy first floor?

Diane is clearly happy that we take the deal.

Not sensing anything specific upon checking into the room, there's still a knowing that something is out of the ordinary as we unpack. Shortly after, we walk around the town but since Ruth is set on getting a reading from someone in the haunted hotel we quickly return. Diane is still behind the small desk to help me make an appointment with Ruth's preferred psychic medium.

Although I don't really feel the need for a reading, I begin to make an appointment for myself with someone else because I don't want Ruth to think that I'm there just for her. I ask that my session be recorded on tape because I tend to live in the Now and easily forget things. There's no sense in having someone "read" for me if I cannot remember what they said. Diane agrees and makes my appointment with Tracey Lightfoot, an Indian woman who specializes in past-life, reiki, and other things.

Ruth is called in for her reading before long and soon after a woman comes to take me to mine. I'm not immediately impressed with the large, short woman who limps as we slowly walk upstairs to her office. It seems that she is not in the best of health, and after sharing my propensity to get into a hot tub of water during cold weather, she talks about how she's too big to get into the bathtub. As we sit in her cluttered office, I ask if she records sessions.

"Well, I did record all my sessions until last night," she replies excitedly. "But during my last session my recorder broke. I can't seem to get it to work now."

"I specifically asked for you because you're the only one in the hotel that records sessions."

Not seeming a bit disappointed, she says she's sorry, totally understands, and we can go back downstairs to get my money back. I think she knows, as I, that we are not quite 'in tune.' I don't want to talk about levels of awareness. This is all an illusion made up in my mind, but clearly, I'm not meant to get a reading from her so we trudge downstairs to get my $100 dollars back.

"Well," I think, "what the heck, there are three areas I could inquire about, health, the book I'm writing, and a spiritual partner." I just want confirmation for those three areas. A spinal thing still seems to be hanging on and it would be nice to be clearer about writing more books. Are they necessary? Should I continue to write? And finally, is there to be a spiritual partner? Since Ruth is still in her session, I decide to walk around town to see if there's someone else who can do a reading.

As I begin to browse shops lining the small street, it occurs to me that my soon to be booked session will be longer than Ruth's reading, so I head back to the front desk, give Diane the room key, and ask her to give it to Ruth when her session is complete. I then move across the street to the Purple Rose for upon our arrival we saw a woman coming out of the building. Alas, they do not record sessions.

People at the next place I choose announce that after having three recorders stolen they took that as a sign that sessions should no longer be recorded. Stubbornly, I move on to the third building where they "used to record but tape cassettes are outdated and now CDs are becoming outdated as well." This establishment is developing a digitalized system where sessions are recorded and sent to clients via email, but the system is not yet developed.

Again sensing a session is not to be; I move back down the street to what is referred to as 'the universal place' to be told that one of the men records sessions. However, he does not have batteries for the recorder today! And, upon inquiring I learn they are not the extra ones carried in my luggage.

"Sorry I can't help you out," he says, as I begin to browse the shelves with merchandise. And then just as I'm ready to leave, he steps in front of me to note, "Oh, but wait, Susan records and she is here today as well."

I book the next session to begin in thirty minutes, but while roaming around the limited gift shop think it's not very nice to hear Susan talking with the person she's 'reading' in another small room. Susan talks about how many children her client will have and what her future will look like.

This does not sound like the kind of reading that I want to have. I know these things. I don't want to say I'm beyond them, but it just does not sound like something that I would want to have done for me.

When it's time for my reading the woman who booked it for me goes to tell Susan I'm there. Surprise, surprise. Susan says, "Oh my, I'm sorry but I can't record the session because I left my tape recorder at home today."

The search is over as I finally get the message; all these signs told me what I already knew. Again, I get my hundred dollars back.

Just as I walk into the hotel Ruth walks out wearing an ugly frown. She's a bit dubious because the psychic/medium repeated everything that I had already told her! Ruth asked certain questions, got the answers, but will not tell me what the questions were.

Her words, "I could have just gone to you," surprise me.

"Yes," I quickly reply, "but it was important that you go to someone that did not know you. That you hear it from a stranger."

"Well, I don't know," Ruth smirks. "She told me things that she could have told anybody."

"Really?" I ask knowing differently. "Oh did she? Did anyone come through?"

"Well, Daniel came through and he told me the same thing that you told me."

"So?"

"The psychic told me that Aunt Mary and Uncle Walter met Daniel when he crossed over to the Otherside."

"Well, there's a bit of information I didn't know."

All in all, I for one am glad my sister got a reading, for as she continues to talk it's clear the information is necessary for her to know.

Ruth's excitement over the prospect of seeing ghosts like the ones in a popular television show soon spills over pasta and beer as we dine at an Italian restaurant several miles away. We buy a disposable camera on the short drive back to our unpredictable adventure so she can take pictures.

A puddle of water sits on the bathroom floor when we return to our room around eight o'clock in the evening. It looks like perhaps someone just stepped out of the shower, only no one used the shower. The tub and area near our toilet is bone dry so I figure it's just a sign to let us know; yes, there is activity in the room. Of course, since Diane told us that the psychic/mediums leave after hours and no one will be back until morning, there's no one to report it to. There's an occupied guest room a few doors down from us, and earlier we saw two girls go into the first room so we know there's at least five people on the first floor. One person, to our knowledge, has a room upstairs

Itching for adventure, perky Ruth wants to roam the now much darker spooky hotel. We should wait until midnight to see the action, like the Ghost Hunters do on television, I announce. Ruth remains adamant about investigating the eerily empty hotel NOW. So we hurriedly walk up the stairs to roam what seems to me an empty second floor. I soon sense unseen spirit energy at the end of the darkened hall near an empty chair and tell Ruth to take a picture. Upon sensing energy at the other end of the hall, I again tell her to take a picture. Yet, we end up going back to our room long before 10:00 PM with Ruth sorely disappointed.

Much to my dismay, as I'm no longer a captive to television, Ruth decides to turn the wall-mounted television on. She watched some kind of murder show for several hours at the last hotel while I kept headphones on, way too loud, listening to prayers and music, trying to drown out any other sound. I could not believe she could watch such a show for three hours, hence revealing the distance in our states of awareness. Tonight will not be a repeat of that experience.

"I don't want to watch any murder shows," I firmly announce as we eat microwaved popcorn. She turns the channel to a show about a medium and a spirit who talks to her. It's not a good spirit and not something that I care to watch, including a torturous scene, and so, again, I put my headphones on after lighting a travel candle.

A creature of habit, as we all are, Ruth rises to take her blue prescription pills when the television show ends. She promptly falls asleep at ten o'clock, thankfully before the usually depressing eleven o'clock news. My headphones remain on while listening to a daily treatment CD, which I am so very grateful to have brought for the trip. Now feeling a bit peeved, I can not believe Ruth is soundly asleep beside me in the large bed while spirit energy becomes denser and denser all around us. Tonight, it is even more important to perform my usual practice of filling myself with Light and, this time, consciously spreading it around the room, encasing the entire suite with love.

The now fully heated suite holds many spirits. As cold creeps through the area, I rise to turn the heat down because our room seems too hot at times. At eleven thirty-five, as Ruth snores next to me, the CD player begins to act erratically. "Perhaps the batteries need to be replaced," I think. "I want to hear my daily treatment CD." I replace the batteries, but the CD player again acts erratically, as it does when Daniel's essence is around. "Clearly," I think, "something is messing with the CD player and it's not Daniel's energy!"

Fear creeps into my awareness so I begin to telepathically talk with the spirits that seem to be coming through a portal by the small sofa to our right a few yards away. "I cannot imagine," I proclaim, "why anyone would pass to the Otherside and not continue on to that wonderful, glorious Light of God. It is one of the things that we come here to do." Adamantly I announce, "Just to feel that wonderful, loving Light! Just to feel the glory of that Light for there is no feeling like it! I just don't understand. How could you possibly want to stay here when that wonderful Light is waiting for you?"

Two entities, in my mind's eye, walk toward the Light. Images of the backs of a tall woman and a little pre-school girl with long, flowing hair fill my brain. The girl's light brown hair glistens as they move into the Light together. As the scene disappears, I smile, with a knowing nod of completion; now uninterrupted music flows easily through headphones into my ears.

It occurs to me to take a picture of the seating area where I sense all the action but the camera sits on a nightstand next to Ruth. She seems to wake easily as I reach for it but drifts quickly back to sleep. I take two pictures as the candle burns on the nightstand nearby.

I continue listening to the CD's calming music, not sensing any more spirits, but filling myself and the suite with love, pumping it out continually. At 3:00 AM, extremely tired because I only slept two hours last night due to the solar energies coming in, I finally turn the CD player off hoping to get some sleep.

But alas, Ruth now begins to make odd noises. She's clearly having a nightmare based on the sounds and jerks of her body. Even when I rest my hand gently upon her shoulder, she continues to sleep. "It's okay," I whisper while starting to rub her shoulder softly. She groans as if being tortured. "Feel love," I whisper. "Just send them love. Just send them love Ruth. Send them love." I don't know why I say it but she immediately quiets down so I can finally fall asleep.

A friendly woman approaches our table as we sit eating the free continental breakfast. She works at the hotel so I ask her what kind of spirit action guests experience in the suite we slept in. She promptly replies the room used to be very active with children.

"I guess," she says with a broad smile, "since it's a big room they like to go there to play. But we have renovated it twice and so there's not as much activity there."

"Well," I say with confidence, "there was a lot of activity last night!"

She listens intently as I describe my experience.

"I'm so glad," she announces with a wide toothy smile. "It's so nice to know that others are ascending into the Light."

One of the greatest reasons we come here is so we can have the wonderful experience of going back into the Light. It is the only time souls can feel the intensity of such a loving, joyous and peaceful experience. And helping someone into the Light by offering them Love, Peace and Joy is the best thing we can do as humans.

Ruth sits quietly with a look of disbelief as she sips her coffee while listening. Before the woman walks away, I tell her about the puddle on the bathroom floor and she again confirms that the hotel, and particularly the room in which we stayed, is eerie.

Bits of what seem like sleet flow from dark skies as Ruth and I walk toward my car. It is very cold and even with my hat and gloves on I am freezing. There is even ice on the windshield and it all takes us by surprise as we scrape the small car's windows. Rain accompanies us almost the entire time we drive to get back home. It stops only as we exit the car to enter my favorite Cracker Barrel restaurant for lunch, and then again as we walk to the car after eating!

Robert Monroe's book *Ultimate Journeys* soon reminds me of my desire to help humanity from the Otherside. It explains why I've helped spirits pass beyond the fourth dimension. Once I'm out of this dense physical form, if still in the same state of mind, I can help many more spirits remember there are many other places to play and learn. We can spiral out of earth life to evolve further in formless states.

PART TWO

Dreams

Dreaming...
What's It All About?

𝔉irst, it's important to note that **where we are when we experience anything at all is in mental space, not physical space**. Aside from brain and memory dreams there are both unconscious and conscious visions reflecting our awareness on what seems as other realms. We may receive messages from higher aspects of Consciousness and experience brain processing of thoughts and daily activities. Processing daily activities is an important point to consider for everything we experience is subject to how the brain chooses to process it. Brain processing includes everything we see with physical eyes, hear with our ears, read, react to, and even things we try to ignore. These things often turn up during the delta state of sleep.

Dreams offer opportunities to experience other aspects of our reality, make changes as desired, and assist us in clearing and transmuting discarnate energies from previous or parallel lives. Multiple lives blend together when we change our state of awareness (vibrational frequency), allowing us to tap into helpful dimensions within time and space.

It's important to note, the clairvoyant gift of precognition may be recognized by one consciously or unconsciously. Truly prophetic dreams, as noted by G. de Purucker in *Esoteric Teachings, Volume 12,* come from the

Reincarnating Ego. Yet knowing that most dreams are irrelevant to daily life, one can choose to ignore them unless upon waking they are remembered as immensely vivid, in which case recording them may be of assistance in the future.

As we and the cosmos continue to unfold, we experience greater heights of BEingness, brought about by our Sun and the Great Central Sun, which is blasting solar winds very high above normal. Normal winds are 300 and 400 km/s (kilometers per second). Cosmic energetics changing our DNA are felt in physical, mental, and emotional bodies as "Light Activation Symptoms," such as profound exhaustion, anxiety, dizziness, head pressure, ears ringing, and strange vivid dreams, which assist us in clearing discarnate cellular records.

We all experience higher realm states of awareness during what is referred to as the 'sleeping state', and need only recall certain words to return to them and bring the teaching to our current state of awareness. For me, tapping into these higher frequencies comes upon waking as the body seems lighter and vibrating in a different state than usual. Enjoy these personal accounts of very vivid dream experiences and make of them what YOU will.

Shared Dream Message

This account of a shared dream is noted within my first book, *THE END OF MY SOAP OPERA LIFE :-) DEATH OF THE SUN.*

Tropical Storm Bonnie makes landfall at 45 miles per hour south of Apalachicola, Florida, while Rebecca and Samantha attend conference meetings. Bonnie's rainfall causes flooding and minor damage that worsens the next day. Category 4 Hurricane Charley moves through Florida on August 13 and hits Punta Gorda harder than any other area. Their family remains safe.

Pictures Rebecca and Samantha take verify, at least for Samantha, that spirits are nearby. Both women feel Daniel's presence strongly at a cocktail reception on the evening that Hurricane Charley moves through Florida. It's the first time they relish in the experience of a New York nightclub.

As in the Keys, Daniel's energy helps Samantha to enjoy herself. She's amazed to drink heavily and joyfully dance, after many years of inactivity, despite multiple

medical conditions. Usually, her face flushes red, with increased blood pressure, despite medication. She often feels short of breath during exercise and her joints ache. Yet, a sudden surge of energy graces her when thoughts of collapsing on the dance floor arise.

Daniel's essence helps both women to stay safe and have a good time. When a man from the conference offers to escort them back to the hotel, Samantha knows it's Daniel's thoughtfulness influencing the helpful stranger. After stumbling down several streets, they crawl into separate beds and quickly pass out.

Both women scream and promptly sit up at 4:00 AM. Samantha, shaking, looks at Rebecca to ask if she had a nightmare. Rebecca quickly answers shaking her small, heart-shaped face to and fro, as if to remove the images.

"Yes, and it wasn't very pretty."

Shock fills them upon relating the same dream. The image of Daniel in a wheelchair, as a quadriplegic like Christopher Reeve, haunts them. Rachel stands behind his wheelchair smiling. Abigail is at his left side with her right hand holding his.

In the dream, Daniel tells them he had a choice after the accident. He chose to leave his physical body. The revelation upsets them greatly as they cry together.

Samantha suddenly recalls reading about dreams that people share of loved ones on the Otherside. Yet, she never imagined it would happen to Rebecca and her, even though they seem more in touch with his soul. They sense *there's a choice to make. Do they choose to stay open to such communications or close themselves off?*

Rebecca chooses the later. "I can't take it anymore Mom," she says with determination wiping tears away. "I have to go back to how I was."

Samantha understands but insists, "I'll never close my mind again. I've seen and experienced too much and know there's something much more to life than anyone believes."

Changing Perspective

Tapping into one's soul plan becomes easier when in the dream state. To acknowledge soul's needs and desires, pay attention to dreams of a somewhat physical nature. In other words, pay attention to dreams in which you may feel threatened or forced into doing something you do not wish to do; pay attention to dreams where you seem to teach or lecture others and be aware that it is yourself bleeding through to relate a long forgotten soul tool in other lives. This is the way to become fully into soul at all times, by remaining asleep while awake and dreaming the circumstances you wish to participate in while asleep.

This will make more sense to you as you tap further into soul purpose and meaning. Know that the seeds of tomorrow are planted today. Each emotion, each thought carries a certain charge. And the charge you give to that emotion and thought builds what you call your future. As noted in this dream recall, Higher Self guidance comes upon asking for it.

Many dreams come during sleeping hours. At 10:30 AM I again ask my Higher Self to remind me of something I'm ready to know. A bus arrives to pick up a man and woman standing by the bus sign in one dream. The man moves forward but the woman hesitates. It is bus number 253 but she is waiting for number 400. Pushing hesitation aside, she finally moves forward to peer into the bus.

The bus driver announces that the number 400 bus could take up to another three hours to arrive. Sweat gathers on the woman's face but she proceeds to wait. The bus driver again speaks, and this time notes it could be up to four hours before the number 400 bus arrives. He finally pulls away as she proceeds to wait.

I witness the scene and think, "My goodness, she is going to stand there and wait. She is going to stand in limitation and wait."

And then I hear there's another way.

"Oh yes," I say. "There's another way. I can pick her up, offer her a ride and show her that thoughts are things and she doesn't have to live in limitation."

"There's always another way," I hear. "You can always choose another way in this world."

Recalling the dream now, I know there is always another way to look at things. When we see something happening there is always another way to look at it. Things here are not as cut and dried as they appear. That's it!

House Hunting: The God Network

Research and viewing time to secure housing of my own before and after receiving proceeds from a divorce settlement are lengthy, covering a period of four months before receiving any funds, but resulting in numerous what some people refer to as "God Network Connections." Time well spent envisioned the perfect healing sanctuary, including a house that is for sale (knowing renters generally do not properly care for rentals and owners would be happy to have their home well cared for until market conditions improve—giving them money to pay taxes and other fees now creating a challenge to meet). Having a house sit empty makes no sense, especially if the electric is off and mold sets in and bugs rule.

Fully prepared to continue purging eons of diagnosed medical conditions—related to the heart, bones, spine, bladder, stomach, bowel and nerves—dozens of homes were physically explored with much disappointment experienced over literal pigsties offered for exorbitant prices (some of which turned out to be God/spirit Network connections). Every home was thoroughly researched on the Internet, avoiding investment companies, for location; building construction; eastern exposure; current and previous owners (passings in the house or attachments to it from previous owners all to be avoided); mortgage status; potential energetic circumstances; local over-development; and water view. Wall colors and, later, possibilities of mold were also considered. While searching for the perfect house, keeping in mind strict requirements, my God Network gift to every real estate agent contacted was advising them to now rent out their clients homes for sale until the market improved.

The following accounts note dreams experienced during house-hunting months in 2007. Some of them were first documented within the pages of my fourth book, *Manifesting: Lightworker's Log.*

House Hunting: Stranger Events

Prayers to continue allowing the actions and words of God to come through me rule while hunting for a house of my own. One of several realtors aware of the search for my decision to rent a house on the market phones on a sunny afternoon to announce that a seller is willing to rent his furnished house for $1,300 a month. "That's out of my price range," I note while calculating expenses and shuddering at the thought of living amid someone else's belongings, "and I don't want a house with furniture."

"What time is best for you to see the owner?"

An afternoon meeting is quickly arranged.

Minutes later I say a silent prayer, as usual while reading *A Course of Miracles*, asking Jesus for my daily words.

"God is ever with you. Do not be afraid."

Dream recall occurs upon waking from a nap before our appointment. At one point in the dream I was trying to get away from some man and as I ran through the streets I looked to my left and my right at every corner trying to decide what way to go. I got to one corner and saw a big archway in the distance. Between the archway and myself was a body of water. There were people in the water and one lady told me it was okay to come in. I saw a man further into the water than the lady who spoke to me. The water was up to his neck and I decided I couldn't go into the water because I was carrying some things that I might lose in the water. I really wanted to get to the archway on the other side but don't recall if I succeeded.

It occurs to me now that the first owners of the house might need a blessing so I bless their souls with everything needed to learn their earth lessons and with increasing never-ending awareness of the One in which we live, and move, and have all BEing.

Another prayer that God's Will continues to be done through me enters my mind along with the usual blessing while driving through neighborhood city streets to avoid major thoroughfares. I'm prompted to open *The Science Of Mind* upon reaching a stop light less than a mile from the house. Remembering that I have not yet read my daily meditation, I open the book randomly to page 340 and am guided to read the bottom meditation, "One With Perfect Action."

"I am One with Perfect Action. Everything that I do, say or think is quickened into action through this right understanding and this correct knowing. The harmonious action of the Great Whole operates through me now and at all times."

"I am carried along by this Right Action and am compelled to do the right thing at the right time."

Overjoyed to read the perfect meditation, I look up from the book to see a fleeting flash of the now familiar Atomic Intelligence, minuscule pinpoints of erratically moving light.

The owner is already at the house and has the side door open but I decide to go up and ring the front doorbell. Four citations from the community association, telling him to fix various things around the property, are tucked into crevices on the door of this house, which obviously needs fresh paint. Not getting a response I walk into the house using the side door.

"Hello, is there anybody here?"

The family room leads to an open kitchen area on the left and the owner, a portly man, two inches taller than I and looking like an unsavory character in a horror movie, appears from beyond it wearing an old white t-shirt with jeans; he looks to be about 65-years-old. I hand him the citations. He quickly shrugs them off saying the association has "a lot of rules."

"The electricity is off so the bell doesn't work," he notes with another shrug upon hearing I'd rung the doorbell. "I have not yet gotten around to fixing the house up for sale," Gary now replies as I look around to see the house is in great disrepair, with numerous little dead bugs on the floors, wallpaper peeling off walls, filthy carpets and needing fresh paint. There is no washer or dryer and really junky furniture, which I have a hard time believing that someone in their right mind would show a house with it there.

"I put the furniture in the house to store it."

Surprisingly, he seems familiar. I'm not uncomfortable around him as we walk through the house to the small bedrooms but am beginning to sense that my purpose is not to rent the house but of something that is much more important.

"Do you know the history of the house?"

"No, I just bought it as an investment."

As a now somewhat savvy house hunter I calmly note, "If you want to know the history of any house you can go onto the Internet to see it."

After I relate the results of my search he admits to buying the home from a lady, who bought it after it was foreclosed on and moved her parents in until he'd bought it several months later.

Changing the conversation, I ask Gary if he knows where the filter is to the air conditioner. He walks right past it with a firm "No," and when I turn to look at him, see and began to take off the vent screws, all the while noting how my mother-in-law had sinus problems and recurring headaches for years before they realized the air conditioning ducts were filled with all kinds of debris. The top of the vent is completely covered with dust and dirt and at this point I know my purpose there is not to rent the house.

"As soon as I can get my guys, I'll be fixing up the house," Gary notes with another shrug.

A familiar closeness to him surprises me as I begin to walk towards the front door while noting that I will not be renting the house. "I need a place that is move-in ready now. My son passed four years ago. Now I'm going through a divorce after being married for twenty years. I don't know if you've ever had someone you love die or not but it changes you."

"Yes, I know. My daughter passed way fifteen years ago."

Clearly my purpose is very much different than originally envisioned, I sense, while knowing his daughter's energy, still stuck in 4D, drew me to the place. "Do you know about the North American Union?"

Gary promptly sits down in a chair with a serious look on his rugged face, across from where I stand, sighs and shakes his beefy head to and fro. Guided by unseen forces, I sit down across from him.

"Well, you might find this odd but ever since my son passed I've felt like he was talking to me."

"Yes, I feel my daughter around sometimes too."

"Do you ever hear her talk to you?"

"No, but sometimes odd things happen and I think she's around then."

"You're right. After my son passed strange things started happening around the house like the television turning on and off by itself."

He leans towards me interested in what I'm saying.

"I started hearing my son talking to me in my head. He told me about things that were going to happen for a long time. I don't hear him as much now but I still feel guided. I've been looking at houses for several weeks now and sometimes I get the feeling that I'm directed to certain houses. I think I'm guided to a certain property not to rent it but for other reasons."

While explaining what I understand about current and future events I note at some point the stock market will crash so it's not a good investment.

"I've never believed in stocks and bonds. I buy houses, fix them up and sell them. I've got forty-two houses right now."

"Well, your daughter wants you to know you're doing the right thing. Maybe that's a way to protect what money you have and you'll be able to rent the houses out because people are not going to be able to afford a house in the future. It looks like your houses are a good investment for you."

Upon feeling the urge to leave there's also an undeniable urge to hug him.

"Do you mind if I hug you?"

"No, not at all."

Now strongly sensing his daughter in the room, I lift my glasses up to the top of my head so they won't interfere and begin to hug him.

"Okay, just stay still."

As his daughter's words come to mind, arms wrap around his body, as far as possible, while pouring out the love within my heart.

"I love you Daddy. Thank you for being such a good dad."

Gary's body relaxes even though I don't say the words out loud. His arms now hug me and I fill with a combination of love, joy and wonder, knowing he feels his daughter's energy and is very grateful. This is her last hug and I am so happy to be the one to help her give it to him physically.

Eyes fill with tears as a flood of emotion overwhelms me. I quickly pull away, thank him and hold out my hand to shake his.

"Thank you for letting me see your house. I have to get to another appointment now."

As he begins to lock the door, I have no doubt that God's Will is done through me. I'm so grateful to be able to help other souls in this way.

House Hunting: Lengthy Condo Saga

𝕴 cannot stress enough the importance of dream recall. Upon opening to greater probabilities, pushing aside worn-out belief systems that never served humanity, one can breeze through this game called life. When a departed family member gives you a gift in a dream, they assure your protection from the Otherside. After such a dream, and signing a lease to move into a reportedly 3.7 million-dollar Intercoastal condominium, I have another 4D adventure.

Upon experiencing weeks of issues with the beautiful, luxurious, exclusive condo, I ask for a refund, having never spent a night there. An account of that experience of learning to trust clairvoyance and intuition is below. Look for the numerous clues as you read it and know, there are always clues to let us know where we do and don't belong.

Day 1: After leaving everything behind for the third time, including husband, home and most belongings, living off a credit card for nearly a year and waiting to finalize the third divorce, plans to finally have my own place instead of staying with my daughter between trips begin to cement as an old friend of my departed son phones to alert me of "a perfect deal."

"This expensive condo sits on the Intercoastal in an exclusive neighborhood," Rita Lynn announces excitedly. "It's a beautifully furnished 2/2 for $1,600 a month but I think that includes everything, electricity, cable, water."

I think about the timing of Rita Lynn's call but also of plans to secure a house in an area less apt to be in the path of a hurricane. Yet, the thought of living in a beautiful condo in a rich area intrigues me even though I'd have to get a storage unit for my few belongings. "Is it on the first floor," I wonder.

So many 'what ifs' fly out the window as I give it up to God after Rita Lynn confesses her dire need for the commission money (realtors usually get a month's rent for securing a year's rental lease). As she talks of setting up an appointment for us to see the condo, I silently agree to listen for inner guidance.

Day 2: "This is the perfect place," Rita Lynn notes, explaining how she just got the listing a day before I emailed her. She has not even put it into the realtor system and it usually costs $3,500 per month. Rita Lynn has successfully assured both the owner's representative and the owner that I am the perfect tenant to care for this home while he goes back to his other house for the summer. And he is now willing to rent the place for $1,200 per month but I'll have to pay my own electric bills.

"As wonderful as it sounds," I calmly reply, "there are several reasons why this deal has more cons than pros for me, including its hurricane path location. My utopia requirements according to other realtors are impossible to meet."

Since Rita Lynn insists the place is perfect for me now, I know it's important to see this condo even if it's just to connect with her, the woman who lived two houses from my son and found a buyer for his small home enabling his small family's last move to a suburban palatial estate, as my family referred to the new much larger home.

Day 6: Having finally secured the condo's keys, Rita Lynn telephones in the late afternoon to ask if I'm available right before sunset. It is then that I learn she is also the realtor of two of my son's other past neighbors, Brian and Gwen, who are friends with the condo's owner.

Since Rita Lynn can't open the door using the key card after we pull up to the Royal Estate building, we walk in through the large garage. Of course, first we go in one main door and out the other to see the Intercoastal and pool area. Although I'm now very conscious about what I put into and on the body, and no longer swim in chlorine-filled water, the expansive waterway beyond a well kept Olympic-sized pool entices. What awesome energy this area holds!

As my little heart begins to pump a bit more quickly, we move back inside the building for Rita Lynn to stop at the first condo door. Alas, the smell of mold assaults nostrils as we walk inside to see huge ceiling to floor windows offering the water-filled view. Expensive furnishings upon shiny wood flooring look new but manly, mainly brown and black, with a large plasma screen television mounted on a wall. The fully furnished condo appears well kept except for a half-full pot of coffee with mold growing in it. Rita Lynn empties it right away thinking the distasteful smell will now dissipate.

Per my usual potential house inspection, I ask her to check the air conditioner's air filter. And as usual, it's overdue to be changed and completely clogged with dust. I look up to see dust on the air vents. "Have the owner check and see when the air conditioning unit was last serviced and cleaned," I ask.

Senses note the condo seems devoid of any noticeable energy. "It's been empty for four months except for short visits from Brian and Gwen," Rita Lynn says. We remain talking for nearly thirty minutes before she returns me to my daughter's house.

Day 7: Rita Lynn now reports that the owner will rent his condo to me for $1,400 per month. The air conditioning was serviced within the year and although his corvette is parked in the garage Rita Lynn will move it so I can park there. Brian and Gwen will move the things from the closets making room for my own clothes and they can get a maid in to clean the place. I'll be doing my laundry in a common coin laundry room.

I remind her that the first of the month is in three days and relay plans to energetically clear and bless the condo before moving anything in.

We can finalize the deal tomorrow, she says, but I need to give her cash for the first month's rent and a security deposit. After that either she or Brian will pick up my monthly rent check on the first of the month. The owner, Bart, is not a real formal kind of guy, but "a hand shake sort of guy" and I'll be staying at the condo as his guest. I will not have to be screened as a renter so that will save me $100-200. This month to month agreement will allow me to move somewhere else if desired.

Day 8: After withdrawing the required amount from the bank, I charge a new filter for the air conditioning system onto my credit card. Rita Lynn takes the day off from her other job so I can get the condo keys earlier than scheduled. Alas, upon entering the condo once again we are assaulted with the acrid smell of mold. Will the new air filter take the scent away? The air conditioning unit is set on 81 degrees so Rita Lynn turns it down.

Assured that all is as it should be, I sign a short agreement that basically notes I am paying $1,400 per month to stay in the condo as a guest. By the time I give her 2.8K in cash, the acrid smell affects me more than it does Rita Lynn. I wonder, knowing it affects the sense of smell, does she smoke? But what a thrill to drive Rita Lynn's new Mustang while she drives Bart's convertible!

Now that the garage spot is open for my 10-year-old car I take my charge card shopping to buy a vacuum cleaner, air purifier and other things that might help get the smell out of the spacious condo before returning to energetically clear and bless it. Unfortunately, the hand-held remote control does not seem to want to open the garage door. I decide to replace the battery with a new one when it finally opens after six tries.

As I enter the condo with a shopping cart from the laundry room filled with my medium-sized red suitcase, food, the new vacuum cleaner and CD player, the acrid smell of mold again disappoints. Surrounding air feels uncomfortably hot. The air conditioner is again set on 81 degrees. After lowering the thermostat, I place baking soda containers in the kitchen, spray the condo with Lysol spray, and fill four ceramic cups part way with bleach to put in different rooms.

Suddenly, I recall a dream nights ago, a more vivid repeat of a dream had last year, and know, I MUST clear this space, release any astral energies, and bless it with the Light of God. With all closet doors open, my new small air cleaner in the master bedroom, and two CD players playing beautiful music, it takes a half hour to bless the house properly and fill it with good energy. An unquenchable thirst upon entering the condo causes me to drink another bottle of water—now making a total of three bottles—before noticing that my head hurts and sinus cavities are beginning to pulse.

Clearly, I cannot stay in the condo for the night. I telephone Bart and thank him for his generosity in letting me stay there, and after asking a few questions, including whether it's okay to take the bedspreads to the cleaners, I tell him about the smell of mold and my attempts to clear it away. "Let me know what happens," he notes before ending our call.

After stripping off bedding in the large, very dusty master bedroom, I notice a small red stain on the brand new pillow top mattress. It looks like a circle of blood maybe an inch in diameter. Dust mites and mold spores do not enter my mind before stripping bedding in the smaller second bedroom so I put my nose down to sniff the bedspread. The gross mistake is clear when my nose stings upon smelling mold and dust for even the bedsack on top of the mattress smells.

After dragging garbage bags of bedding to the shopping cart, I move into the bathroom to see an air vent filled with dust. I turn over the wastebasket with its $19.95 price tag, and thankful to see it's made of heavy metal set it down under the air vent, knowing it will hold my weight. Exhaustion sets in after wiping at the dust and green mildew clinging to air vents so I decide to clean all vents on the next visit.

Minutes later with a pounding head that feels as if it's going to explode, amid pulsating sinus cavities, I gladly accept my daughter's offer of hot chicken soup, but before finishing the meal crawl into bed.

Day 9: After rising throughout the night, still ill, I get up in the afternoon to notify Rita Lynn who sounds quite surprised. Thirty minutes after our short call, she phones to tell me to stay away from the place for a few days. Brian and another man will go to the condo to clean the vents and make sure everything is okay. Not happy about the situation, Rita Lynn advises me to telephone my doctor, tell him I've been in a dusty situation and need an antibiotic. It's difficult to do since I've avoided him for two years.

Later in the day while picking up my prescription, I shutter to think of Bart's condo being ruined because of a faulty air conditioning system. I truly believe I've been guided to the condo for the good of all concerned.

Day 10: Rita Lynn assures me via phone that Brian will "take care of everything" and if I miss any time in the condo Bart will prorate the rent. "That," I note still in bed, "is the least of my concerns, but don't worry I'm now taking Zithromax." Something then prompts me to ask her to reconnect with my daughter-in-law who is now distanced from everyone familiar. She gladly agrees.

Day 11: Sinuses are still blocked but my head no longer hurts as I slug down a probiotic drink before returning to bed.

Intuition is the Seventh Insight discussed in *The Celestine Prophecy*. It becomes much easier to be led by intuition as you become more clear of who you are. Staying connected to our Higher Self is the best thing we can do. And it's always good to find "the silver lining in every event, no matter how negative."

Later, Rita Lynn phones to note Brian "cleaned everything up" so it's okay to move into the condo. Intuition tells me the mold smell is still apparent and I know the air conditioning ducts need to be cleaned if not replaced. Having dealt with mold issues before I know sometimes everything made of fabric can carry mold spores until properly cleaned.

Rita Lynn now sounds upset noting someone has to be at the condo to let in the air conditioning guy. I again remind her that my renting the condo was the win-win situation that I'd prayed for. "It's such a beautiful place," I note. "I'd hate to think what might have happened if I hadn't been led there and the mold situation got worse."

"Well, you move at your own pace and do what you what," she says, "but it's ready to move into now."

"I'll stop by the condo after dropping off the bedspreads at the cleaners," I reply.

Once again the condo's garage door opener does not seem to work. Figuring I must have replaced the battery wrong, I pull into the parking lot a few feet away to enter the main door. Other thoughts distract me. How cool is it to walk down the hall looking at the Intercoastal to the only condo door? And then I unlock both locks with great anticipation, but am disappointed to smell the mold again. Not risking another major headache, I pack up my case of CD's, morning cereal, house blessing tools, and my open box of Kleenex and walk back to the bedrooms to find that Brian left the door to the master bedroom open. My air cleaner is working away but it's not doing its job with all the open doors so I close the master bathroom door, the walk-in closet door and the door to the bedroom. It occurs to me to get a stranger to come in and tell me if they smell anything.

As I start to lock up the condo, I see a woman on the other side of the door pressing a button to gain entrance into the building. I quickly walk over, let her in, and ask if she will do me a favor.

"Sure, what do you need?"

I ask her to follow me to the condo down the hall to see if she can smell any mold. I'm happy to be a guest of the condo's owner, I note, but it smells like mold inside to me and I can't stay there.

"Oh, this is a very beautiful place," she soon says taking a few steps into the room. "I love the view. Yes, it does have like a wet smell. It smells kind of moldy. I have sinus problems and can still smell it."

I thank her, and as she walks back out the door, she wishes me luck.

Resigned, I sit comfortably in my air conditioned car to phone Bart with an update. He listens as I relay repeated prayers for a win-win housing situation. Brian will resolve the issue, he assures, as I again tell him what a beautiful place it is.

Day 13: I wake from a vivid dream involving color to feel eyes moist with tears.

While in a house that looked like a condominium (the majority of living situations have been in houses), I turned on the light to see a few spots of what looked like green grime on the wall to my left, in three places.

I began to spread my light, but something seemed to try and control my body as I started to bless the bathroom. My body began to shake uncontrollably wobbling back and forth as if energy were trying to enter it. I then realized something bad had happened in the bathroom, perhaps a death, and I had to also clear it of negative energies, so I turned around to go back upstairs to get my white candle and the rest of my 'clearing stuff'.

The next thing I remember is seeing Grandpa coming into the door from across the room on the right hand side. He wore the usual faded brown suit, stood directly in front of me about nine feet away, and carried a large brown bag in his arms that was a house warming gift for me. Perhaps my cousin with whom he lived had brought him over to see me, I thought.

So very happy to see him, I joyfully ran across the room to put my arms around him. Grandpa asked me how I was. I began to cry as I hugged him tightly saying, "Oh Grandpa, I love you. I haven't seen you in such a long time." I sensed he had something to tell me, but then I remembered he had died; he lived to be 100-years-old and died a few days later. As I continued to joyfully hug him pouring love into his body, my own body violently shook back and forth. Grandpa wants to tell me something, but again, my emotion blocks the message and I wake with tears rolling down both cheeks.

The dream reminds me of a similar one experienced exactly one year before, of being in a condo, moving into the basement to bless it and then starting to shake uncontrollably. Something bad happened in the basement bathroom so I go back upstairs to get my blessing tools. Grandpa is upstairs wearing his brown suit. I start crying with joy and hug him. After asking how he is, I fill his body with love. My body shakes while holding him. He wants to tell me something. But emotion gets in the way and I wake with tears rolling down cheeks. Obviously, the key to receiving messages from departed loved one's is to remain detached upon seeing them to avoid waking before messages occur.

Now unable to imagine God putting me in a place where I might be in harm's way, I decide to go with the flow and see if the condo is my temporary place to live until I find the perfect house. Internet information on the condo's owner reveals he is either a successful entrepreneur or a gangster who buys and resells properties frequently here in South Florida. In any event, I am to have some kind of interaction with this man. Only earth time will disclose the reasons but I'm letting this go knowing God will take care of things for me.

Day 14: Moldy smells greet my teenage grandson and I when we stop by the condo after school. Scrutiny reveals that a man used the bathroom for the toilet seat is left up. The air conditioning vents are wiped but not cleaned the way I would clean them and the fabric shower curtains need to be washed. Thankfully, the master bedroom door, walk-in closet door and master bathroom door are closed so my new air cleaner can work properly. Dust on wooden shades alerts me to the fact that everything else needs a good cleaning, including rugs on the floor, tub mats, and towels hanging on racks.

A neighbor notes the building has some flooding in the basement during storms but it's never deeper than a foot or so. Yet, there's missing molding near the back door. Bart does not answer his phone when I call him with my latest report.

Day 15: Bart phones to report that Brian will be at the condo tomorrow with the air conditioning man and a machine to rid it of any moisture that might be in the air. It seems as if he wants to be certain his condo is as perfect as can be and says he'll phone again to let me know when I can return there. Obviously, the rent will start at a date later than our signed rental agreement.

Day 16: Sinus cavities still feel stuffy and my head hurts so I phone my doctor for another round of antibiotics. Since I took the last antibiotic two days ago but still feel sinus congestion and pain, the receptionist notes they'd phone in another prescription for me.

Day 17: Now I'm now on Cipro that makes me tired and I have to be diligent about eating, warding away gastric distress, and assuring that yeast doesn't grow where it's not supposed to grow. Rita Lynn phones and after hearing my update notes that Brian is having a hard time getting the scheduling right but will "take care of it today."

I am a bit confused now for it sounds like either Bart has not talked with Brian or Brian has an issue he's not taking about. Rita Lynn is adamant about finding out what is going on as she now feels personally responsible. I can sense wheels moving in her mind as she calculates the rent money I've already paid to stay there. "Things happen as they should and I have full trust in Bart," I confess.

Before ending our conversation, we discuss air conditioning issues and the rampant dust on window blinds, which probably got there due to the dirty air filter.

Rita Lynn telephones me back within an hour to report everything has been taken care of at the condo. The broken thermostat is replaced and Brian says he cleaned all air vents and the smell is completely gone.

Twenty-five minutes later, upon entering the condo my excitement wanes with the smell of mold. Three new pretty pillows on the brown suede couch catch my eye but I don't let them distract me while walking over to the back door to see the missing molding has not been replaced. Although the air conditioning thermostat has been replaced, the air monitor unit near the door reads 84 degrees with 48% humidity. I now decide to take off the air vent in the bathroom to see if it has indeed been cleaned.

Several tiny hairs sit on the back of the toilet behind the seat. I try to ignore them while turning over the new metal wastebasket before setting it down under the air vent. Lacking a Phillips screwdriver I know the tiny blade on a corkscrew from the kitchen will work. After standing on the metal wastebasket, I unscrew the two screws holding up the vent from the ceiling and am amazed at how easy they loosen as I pull the vent toward me; a little furry of dust drifts to the floor. The air vent is lined with dust and that's all I need to see before putting the two screws and the air vent on the bathroom counter and leaving the condo to phone Rita Lynn.

When she quickly answers her telephone, I immediately apologize for calling her and ask for advice on what to do. Does Brian have a drinking problem? When the answer is "No" there's only one thing left to do; call Bart and tell him even if I feel like a tattletale.

Bart also answers his telephone quickly and I again note how beautiful his place is and how it would be a shame to see it ruined because of dirty air ducts. "I'll call Brian right away," he says.

I'm beginning to be concerned that Brian has a key to the condo and now think it might be better to get him out of the picture, but I don't know the extent of their relationship. Is Brian his handyman? I ask myself.

"So, you want me to just speak with you?" I ask Bart.

"Yes."

"Okay, then. I'll wait for your call."

Day 18: Today my nose is more stuffed up than it has been for a day or so and I'm extremely tired, unable to keep my eyes open. So what is the lesson to learn from this experience?

Day 19: Brian, Bart now reports, has cleaned out all the air vents and cleaned up the condo and it's ready for me to live in. I thank him and with a somewhat skeptical attitude say I'll go to the condo to check it out. It just seems to me that if air conditioner ducts need cleaning it should be done by a professional and licensed specialist.

Eight pushes on my garage door opener finally allow entry to open the gate and park my car. When I enter the condo the smell of musty mold fills my nostrils again. It's disappointing but I decide to stay and check the AC vents myself.

Back door molding still has not been replaced, leaving a crack in the door for moisture to enter during the upcoming rainy season. Dust falls to the floor when I open some AC vents and in the bathroom vent two rocks fall to the floor. Alas, all five checked AC vents look mainly clean but there's still dust to see. A moist piece of paper towel in each air duct comes up with dust every time. The wall nearest to the second bedroom vent is covered in dust that clings to it half way down to the floor and halfway to the window on the other side of the room. NOW I am utterly disgusted.

It upsets me to think that such an expensive and beautiful condo will be ruined if it is not cared for properly. In a calm voice, I tell Bart that I'm beginning to think that maybe his place is not where I'm supposed to be.

"I just don't know what to do at this point."

"I'll call Brian and we'll get it taken care of," Bart replies. "If you're not happy with the place, we'll fix it."

I again stress that my being happy isn't the issue; it's important to make sure his beautiful place is not destroyed and I really need a place to heal.

Bart reassures me again that everything will be taken care of, so, resigned, I agree to wait for his next phone call even though it's clear that Brian is not capable of doing what needs to be done, and his work is not up to standard. Bart's insistence on depending on Brian to fix things up after repeated failures to do so disturbs me. Yet, I shall wait for things "to unfold" as guided. God and spirit work in mysteriously wonderful ways and I'm a pawn in a dream world that I myself made up. If I'm just meant to spend some time helping Bart to protect his investment property then something better is waiting for me. I don't know where it is or what it looks like, but I know it's a perfect place for me.

Day 20: Leonardo, a general contractor I know from church comes to mind as I wake up on Sunday morning. Intuition guides me to ask for his advice on the mold issue so when our service ends I ask for a few minutes of his time. "It doesn't matter if it's green mold or black mold," he says. "It's all a health issue. You can't stay in the place no matter how exclusive it is."

Saddened, I leave, determined to clear my things out of the condo. God will give me the strength needed to haul out the vacuum, new telescopic mop, cleaning supplies, CD player and hurricane food. It again takes eight pushes of the remote door opener to open the main gate.

The smell of mold again soon fills my nostrils as I hurry from room to room. One house blessing CD is missing from my new player in the living room and my CD of piano music is missing from the second bedroom CD player. I just shrug it off and with hardly a look at the beautiful view outside the ceiling to floor living room windows go out the door.

Before pulling out of the parking garage, I telephone Bart to leave a short message, noting I've taken my things from the condo and my contractor friend says it's an unhealthy place to be in with the mold. I again stress that he needs to have the air vents cleaned professionally and the house professionally cleaned of mold too.

Bart phones as I'm walking through the grocery store to report that Brian will try and get an air conditioning guy out to the condo tomorrow. "I'm now on my second course of antibiotics and just don't think I can live there," I say. "It's unhealthy and now in all the fabrics." Maybe, I have just finished up some past karma, I silently think.

Day 23: Bart phones to excitedly report that "the condo is all cleaned up" and according to Brian, "smells wonderful. I'm having Stanley Steamer come out tomorrow and I'd very much appreciate it if you could stop by there this afternoon because I value your opinion."

With a great deal of resignation I agree.

It's after 2:00 PM and I really do not want to go to condo alone. Every time I go it's now a reminder of what I could have had. Yet, I must remember, this condo was offered so I could be sure that a more luxurious lifestyle is what I truly want. I phone to see if my sister and her tourist friend will come as well. We soon head to the condo amid perfect South Florida temperature, watching puffy white clouds float amid blue skies, as I apologize for the back seat of my car is half full of belongings; the trunk has been full of personal things for months.

After pressing the battery-operated gizmo ten times, I note it's a sign this is not my place. A woman sitting on the porch at the entrance takes pity on me and motions for me to put my window down. "Are you having trouble opening the garage gate?" she asks. "Maybe you just need a new battery."

"I just replaced the battery."

She takes the gizmo from my hand and clicks it twice; the gate opens. "It's this big button."

"Yes I know. You must have the magic touch."

She smiles, shrugs, hands me back the remote and walks back to the porch steps to sit.

As soon as the condo door opens we all remark about the smell of mold. I lead them room by room through the condo pointing out the same dirty things seen before. Dust still lines walls of the second bedroom and the fabric shower curtains are still stained having not been washed. Pubic hairs are on the bathroom floor and that's all I need to see. As I lock the condo door behind me I'm glad to have blessed the space.

I show my sister and her friend the view outside before we leave and as they take it all in I telephone Bart to note what we've seen and ask for my money back.

"Sorry things didn't work out, I'll get with Rita Lynn and send you out a check," he says.

Since I gave Rita Lynn 2.8K in cash that's what I should get back, I think, but I don't argue the point knowing that another God mission is complete.

Day 24: Rita Lynn phones later in the afternoon to try and talk me into moving into the condo. In a strong and determined voice I note my latest 'condo saga' and say the saga is over and I just want my money back.

Day 30: Rita Lynn phones to say Bart really thinks the condo is okay for me to move into. He's had the air ducts cleaned professionally by Stanley Steemer.

Perception is a wonderful thing and I can see everyone's side of the 'saga'. I again describe the whole saga and remind her that I've just been through almost a month of mental and physical trauma. And if I was a different kind of person I would be thinking about getting some kind of restitution. Then I explain that I'd been directed to the condo for three reasons. One was to help Bart save his condo from further mold damage. Another was to try and reconnect her with my daughter-in-law, and the third was to alert someone about Brian's poor perception. He either has to be an alcoholic or a drug addict because his perception is way off. His perception, if it is his perception and not Bart's instructions, reminds me of how my crack addict brother acts.

Rita Lynn has spent her commission and doesn't know how she is going to get the $700. She asks me to check the condo out one more time. She wants to see the place again but now doesn't have a key. Will I give her my keys? I tell her when I get my money back she can have the keys. She is not happy to hear that if Bart wants me to check out his place, I'll do it as a favor for him, to let him know if anything else needs to be done, but I still want my money back. And if I smell mold when we enter the condo it will be a very short visit. "I'll call Bart again," Rita Lynn says with a low voice.

Day 32: Upon telephoning Rita Lynn to see what the status is on my refund, I'm told she has now "certified the condo as being free of mold." I wonder how she did that since when I spoke to her two days ago she said she had no way to enter the condo and wanted my keys to check it out. Now I remind her that I gave her all of my cash, charged $71 to get the bedspreads dry cleaned, charged the new air filter, air purifiers, air fresheners and antibiotics and have two missing CD's. She cannot imagine why Brian would take the CDs and neither can I but he is the only other person with a key that had access to the condo, as far as I know. She then tells me to call Bart. Without any cash and a rapidly growing credit card balance I have no choice.

Bart kindly notes he will call Rita Lynn to resolve the matter. He'll send a check next week but it has to go to Rita Lynn because that's how it's done.

I have invested a lot of precious time into this saga and it has been taxing on my physical, emotional, and mental health. Yet, I'm grateful to have been able to help Bart avert what could have been a much more serous situation with his lovely condo. Because the realtor and Brian were both friends of my son who died in 2004, I think there are more reasons I was guided there too. I now feel a short note to Bart along with detailed journal entries will help to avoid further issues.

The older I get, the more I realize that sometimes things may not be as they first appear. I bless Bart with prosperity and success and thank him for the opportunity to learn, and silently, for the lessons of patience and maintaining composure in the midst of chaos.

Paying attention to unexpected delays, coupled with clairvoyance and intuition, leads to a less strenuous life. Finally, two months later, Rita Lynn finds the perfect very well maintained, extremely large 2/2 house with hurricane shutters, a master bedroom walk-in closet, Florida room and den that exceeds stringent requirements. With updated kitchen and baths, tile floors throughout except for the desired carpet in bedrooms, new air conditioning, large screened back porch, shaded back patio, and a wide canal view with no neighbors behind it; the estate sits securely on an obscure street in an age 55 and over community. It also boasts a good roof and windows, garage with washer and dryer, stainless steel appliances and a reverse osmosis water filter.

Dreams While In the Perfect 2/2

Before falling asleep on a cooler mid-March day, while living in my first residence alone for the very first time at 57-years-old, I ask to remember being on another realm. My desire is met six hours later upon waking to remember being in a beautifully exquisite place, like a pristine national forest.

The land was so fertile, so picturesque, as I started at the beginning of the park with everyone else. At first we were all in our own vehicles; I don't know what kind of vehicles they were. But soon I rode with two other people in their vehicle. We were going along the usual path and all of the sudden the tall, dark-haired male driver said "hang on." Up we went over a very small beautiful hill, kind of jumped up on it, and the very fertile, green and absolutely, stunningly, indescribably beautiful land before us took my breath away. As the vehicle landed on lush, fertile, dark green grass to my left a beautifully well hidden cave in the bottom of one of the mountains stood out; that's where the excited driver was headed. Some kind of animal, a cow, or other kind of big animal stood in back of our vehicle ready to be let loose to find its own way.

To my right, in the distance, a man who appeared middle-aged stood caring for another smaller animal. Tall, with delicate features and dark long hair, he looked up to see us with mild curiosity. For a moment, I thought he might stop us, but he didn't. When his eyes glazed into mine I asked him if the animal would be okay on its own. "Oh yes, he'll be just fine," the smiling man said with a knowing nod of his small head.

At that point, I announced that I could not go further on to the beautiful cave. "I have to make my own way. I have to go back the original way."

I don't know why I had to "go back the original way" or why I had to leave them, but they understood.

Minutes later while pondering the dream a message popped into my brain:

"Let me forget the patterns of exclusion as I move forward in time to its end."

Tapping Into Future Lives

As our frequency rises during sleeping hours, sometimes we tap into what seems as future or past lives to receive guidance. We can use the information to bring long forgotten gifts and talents into the current life, avoid harm either experienced in past lives or potentially in the current life, or follow clues to lead us to greater soul evolution in other ways. In 2011, I woke from sleep remembering another more evolved aspect of myself, living in another time and space.

In this other life, I was sitting and listening to someone talking about a meeting in a Penthouse, while someone else asked the man sitting next to me if he was having the meeting that evening. He turned so I could see him and replied, "Yes." We began to talk. He said there was something wrong with his left hand, around his wrist. I held it and it instantly healed. As he walked out the door, he asked if I was coming to the meeting. I answered yes and showed him the number seven.

I transcribed this after booking my arrival in AZ on 11-7-11, three days before a Lightworker meeting in Scottsdale! So, to me, this was a heads-up that I would again be with those from yet another of my soul's lives. My departed son's first love that lives near the meeting location had just reconnected with me through Facebook, after, of course, Daniel's energy guided me to ask her to be my "friend." She picked me up at the airport! During our two times together, I relayed messages and made it possible for the three of us to achieve the healing of closure. Also, to add more to the joy of closure Alfred, who played a life-affirming role in not only my son's life but mine as well, shared our last meal together.

Pay attention to your dreams and keep a bedside pad or recorder to document them. They may not hold meaning initially, but at a future time, especially when it's time to evolve, they will make perfect sense.

A Heads-Up As To Future Events

Precognition is a gift of clairvoyance that can be a warning or heads-up as to what is to occur. Tapping into this gift one may quell concerns about the future and/or be assured that future events can unfold to one's liking, or not, depending on the response during an actual physical experience. In any event, the clairvoyant gift of precognition may be recognized by one accustomed to tapping into higher aspects of ones Self. Left unrecognized, it is what may be referred to as a wasted gift.

In June of 2019, I woke from a dream of being in a urinary medical project in which my daughter (who transitioned on 12-4-15) and the doctor suggested I have a certain test. I said, "Wait a minute, let me check in with my Higher Self." Then I said, "No I don't need this. This is a sick-care system. You can put down that the patient refused. You can put down that the patient is against the A.M.A. (American Medical Association). You can put down whatever you want."

The person that was in charge of recording this interaction said, "Okay" and began writing.

"Be careful about what you write down because we need more patients in this study," said the adamant doctor.

"Just deal with it because you know there's one in every bunch," I calmly replied while grinning widely.

The dream was of a medical trial like the one I pondered about participating in many years ago when diagnosed with an incurable condition, facing the option of getting a pig's bladder to replace my own. And at one point, my doctor had me sign a waiver to free him from responsibility, saying I was against A.M.A. Guidelines and was not following his advice. Obviously, I changed that timeline, by refusing to have the experience of a clinical trial participant getting a pig's bladder!

In 2020, it becomes apparent this was a precognition dream, giving a heads-up of things to come as global testing began with two so-called 'vaccine' shots, which many people unknowingly took to became test subjects. Sensing the illogical stream of so-called 'facts', without remembering this heads-up, I declined to enter that steam of consciousness.

Upon recognizing our True Nature, we must then be aware of other states, other bands of consciousness and be aware of what is occurring in these bands. This does not mean that we need to participate, unless our soul prompts us to do so, but to be aware that there are aspects of ourselves moving through the experience of earth life, as we, yet at different states of awareness. As conscious beings, aware of our own soul plan and purpose on earth, we must allow all experiences without interfering, unless our Higher Self prompts us to do so.

Changing Physical Reality While In The Astral Realm

Lucid Dreaming: Changing Timelines

Changing timelines merely means changing what one experiences. One of the ways we can do this is through what we refer to as our dreams. I continue to wake remembering dreams and sometimes go back in to change them. For instance, if I recall a dream where someone was treated badly by anyone I will drop back off to an altered state and return to the dream to tell them it is not the way to treat people. So, sleeping more does have its usually unknown benefits, as we are doing much more than we may be aware of during periods of rest. We are working in the Astral Realm of Consciousness to change reality in our physical world. The following is an account of how we build our world with emotion and thought.

Today's waking dream was one where I manipulated the energy of a tornado in the distance. Upon seeing it far away, I became fearful watching it expand, becoming denser and darker. Then I realized I might be able to control it with emotion and fed it love instead of fear. The tornado became smaller and lighter in color before I again fed it with fear to watch it expand. Just to be sure of the results, I did this three times over the course of about six minutes. And then I began to tell two young disbelieving men and a woman what I had done and note it was possible for them to do this as well.

After having this dream I shared it two-weeks later during a class titled "Manipulating Energy Consciously." Read about a tornado experience in Tamarac, FL, eight years later, named *"Anchoring Energy,"* in Part Four on page 139.

Lucid Dreaming:
Parallel Multidimensional Living

𝕳umanity continues to move through waves of increased frequencies that are very strong, and along with other signs of a changing body many people sleep much more. Currently for me, sleep is inescapable, in numerous bouts, for ten to twelve hours during the night with a one to three hour nap after brunch near noon! During the nighttime, I'm now consistently reaching higher frequency dimensions, one journal entry of which is related below.

So if this is a dream world of our own making and we continue to return out of habit, obviously the way out is to change habits. The habit changed within the dimension of this next sleep time was of disbelief of the power to move through what appears as solid objects. In this dream dimension, the location seemed to be Tibet with lighter, gold colored houses featuring beautiful gold trim and fascia. A moving train and a moving house appeared before me. The train looked as the houses, but slimmer and moving on tracks. The house was much wider and taller and moved along with the train but it was on the ground. And then they both seemed to adjust easily down into the ground, but not all the way; they kept their fluid movement forward, yet more of the train and house seemed underground. They then moved back up making the train and house more visible above ground.

Now I seemed to be moving with the house, and as the house moved, it began to flow through what seemed as solid gold-colored walls. Upon approaching the first one, I reminded myself to go with the flow and was guided to just close my eyes and not react. The key to moving through walls was to know you could and not hold any fear or denial of the ability to do so; as I moved though several walls along with the house, each one seemed a bit denser and darker.

Within the same month the experience below occurred as I consistently asked to remember being in dimensions where I'm more conscious than I seem to be in this one. Note that the collage of dreams often includes every day happenings, which our brain processes during sleep.

WOW! I was in bed, on the cusp of waking, moving in and out of dimensions, and at one point in a dream where my friend and I seemed to be at our favorite thrift store, but we were at work, scanning shelves of sale items to look for needed materials. One of the things we were looking for was napkins and as I looked at the shelves of napkins, a number of beautiful, ivory-colored linen napkins caught my eye (Several years ago, I gave away such beautiful, nearly brand-new napkins.) I thought they were nice and perhaps I should take one home with me. One napkin was marked $5 in black permanent marker and I thought that stupid, thinking the napkin was ruined and no one would purchase it with the price marked on it. Upon closer inspection, I saw that the $5 price was marked onto a wide piece of tape that was taped (I taped something before bedtime) to the napkin so the linen was not destroyed. So then, I thought I'd take one of the napkins because it would look nice in my place. Then I forgot what I was doing and asked myself, "Wait a minute, what was I doing?"

My friend now seemed gone and I tried to get back to the napkins but all of the sudden I seemed to be sucked out of the room, backwards. The scenery kept changing, my body kept moving, and I couldn't control it; I was being sucked out of scenes and kept moving, flowing faster and faster, faster and faster watching scenery. At one point, I began to panic.

"Wait a minute. What's going on here? What's happening?"

Then I told myself, "Just go, and just go with the flow."

Now I seemed to be the Witness, just watching scenery without emotion, moving towards something, no longer backward but able to see what I approached; still being pulled forward, as a brilliant, golden-yellow wall of Light materialized way ahead of me. The wall was not well-defined but seemed to morph into the scenery from which I was coming from. It was a very fluid coming together of golden-yellow Light and scenery. It *appeared that once you reached the Light there were degrees of Light, deeper and deeper shades of Light to move into.*

I continued to flow towards the Light, but before I reached the Light a noise within the dimension where my physical body lay in bed caught my attention. It was the movement of bedroom vinyl window blinds. My mental body then had to determine how that noise woke me because the windows were closed and, I thought, there was noting to rustle the blinds. But then upon opening my eyes, I realized that a cloth lay at the bottom of the blinds (to block out harsh lighting from outside during the night) and it had fallen off, causing blinds to waver and wake me with the noise.

Of course, right away I grabbed the tape recorder to document this grand experience! Hopefully, next time there will not be anything to pull me out of that dimension and I shall complete the experience. It was a good, wild experience!

Serving Prisoners

Dawn breaks as I remember being in another realm visiting someone in prison during visiting day. Since I've had this experience, numerous times in this life, having visited Saul who later became husband number two, I pay attention to details as they now arise. It was a very vivid dream and a much better experience than I ever had on this realm when I went to visit Saul.

A crisp twenty dollar bill sat in my hand in this very vivid dream and I was going to put it into his account (something I had done during visits nearly forty years earlier). My heavy wool coat almost fell to the floor while switching it to the other arm as I stepped toward the counter to be signed in, while getting the required driver's license out of a jeans pocket at the same time. Many people of different genders, ages and backgrounds moved through the somewhat large room and winter coats were flung on chairs.

The lady behind the counter told me about a new program the jail started for prisoners. You could have prison guards say anything you wanted the prisoner to hear every morning. She said some people were making recordings of what they wanted to say.

"Well, what do some people say?" I asked.

"Some people say they want to have sex with them and make love with them but others, some are inspiring."

I then looked at an informational sign with suggestions for the new program. "We suggest a combination of two or three of these." I recall seeing: "I make the world with my thoughts; I am the light of the world; You are powerful beyond belief." You can also make beautiful inspiring songs or an inspiring affirmation that the prisoner will hear every morning.

Simply delighted and smiling widely, I thought it was a wonderful idea.

In a flash, I was now sitting on top of a very high place, watching a prisoner wearing a white apron walking way down below; the apron was untied in the back. The prisoner looked up at me and telepathically asked if I would come down and help him with his apron. He didn't use spoken words but his eyes because he knew he was being watched by the guards. I thought he had something to tell me so I got off of my ladder and went down, but he walked slowly away. When the apron started to fall I said, "Here, let me help you with your apron." A guard in white stepped up as soon as I started to tie it around the prisoner's back. He just stood watching as I tied the apron. I turned my head to the left and looked at him. "May I help you sir?" I politely asked.

"No," the brusque guard said quickly, "I'm just making sure that so and so is okay." (I can't recall the name he said). Turning to face the tall, thin inmate he then spoke in what, for him as a guard paid to keep people in line, was surely a forbidden concerned manner. "You know, you need to take care of yourself. You have a hundred and four degree fever."

He then said other things but I don't recall them.

As I continued to tie his apron, heat rose from the prisoner's body where uncovered flesh was apparent. "You know, you do feel hot," I said.

"Yeah, I do?"

That's when I woke up feeling the usual body heat (experienced during times of increased geomagnetic activity) to gulp down nearly a bottle of spring water before closing my eyes, returning to the astral realm, and again envisioning an inspiring morning wake-up message for the prisoner.

Changing Community Behaviors

While reading *Conscious Dreaming* I wake one sunny morning to recall being with a conscious group of leaders acting as role models.

We all sat together in a very large, colorful arena ready to watch a show on the stage many sections of rows below us. As our excited crowd waited for the performance to begin, an angry man, many rows in front of our seats, forcefully pushed the shoulder of a woman he was facing, as if to shove her off her seat so she'd tumble down the arena stairs. Her unconcerned face, as if his action was ordinary, caught my attention while noticing she wore a baby blue scoop-necked top. I got the impression she was his wife and gasped loudly along with several people around me. Numerous members of the audience then did the same thing before we all got up and walked silently out of the packed arena. It was a stunning and meaningful message for the man that his behavior was not appropriate as most of the audience then also silently walked out of the arena.

Clearing and Transmuting

What a wild ride! On many nights, I ask my Higher Self to help me purge whatever is left that needs to be transmuted, and upon waking in a new king-sized bed know it's accomplished. One night, shortly after a trip to Brazil to see John of God, I'm taking in Light while balancing a new, small wooden triangle upon my forehead. I then hear to sleep because I've taken in a lot of Light.

Two hours later, I wake after having numerous dreams of purging many, many things. People were chasing me through a house in one dream where I hid in a closet and then sat upon a bed to meditate before they found me. "Why are you chasing me?" I asked.

"I want to kill you."

"Don't you know there is no death? These are just temporary bodies that are housing our spirit so that *All That Is* can experience more."

In another sequence, a small number of people including myself were selling things, like at a garage sale. It was crazy time, and at one point, there was a woman outside crying that she was alone. I went outside and brought her into the house. She had a gun and was going to kill herself. I took the gun, noticed it was cocked and loaded, and broke it, somehow, trying to disarm it. I then told her I would buy her a new one. The gun then turned into a video camera.

"I've been through a lot of shit," I confided, before revealing a scary experience where Saul held a loaded gun to my head while screaming, "If I can't have you, nobody can."

Upon waking, I proceed to give that memory up to the Light, all the fear, the violence, everything negative that happened in my life. Once again, I give it all up to the Light of God, filling now empty spaces with more Light. Traumatic memory after memory dissolves into Light as I consciously give them up.

Continuing to move through this clearing process on a daily basis, I transmute and purge everything not for the higher good, consciously while awake, and even during what appears as dreams; it is good to rid myself of all karma, to balance experience and expression, and to never need return to separation and duality!

Dreams Foretelling Future Events

We all receive information on future events during sleep, whether we realize it or not. The following journal entries are examples of such dreams giving me a heads-up on not only my soul's mission in this lifetime but where I shall live. Keep in mind, while dreaming the brain processes past events even while our Higher Human Soul Self burrows through frequencies to alert us of information on various subjects.

Still unsure if moving will be necessary on April first, I wake from a dream on March 22, 2012. I was with James, again, I think, in another illusory timeline. We were separated but driving a young Samuel to school. They listened as I announced plans to teach something to several different levels, audiences, elementary school, middle school, and high school.

People wore a double chain around their neck. One chain had a golden heart and the other held a silver ingot. (I took my Brazilian crystal heart from its silver chain and put it with the gold ingot and gold chain bought while in Egypt, to wear during a later cruise, and I continue to wear it.) James thought the double chain was mine, but I said, "No, it must be Rebecca's."

There were also two more chains, but again I said, "No. They must be Rebecca's. They're not mine."

We dropped Samuel off, and at one point James stood stiffly, determined to remain detached, as my arms wrapped around him for a hug.

"'I guess I'll have to move to North Carolina," I said matter of factly. "That will be the best thing for both of us as individuals."

Ten days after the dream, on April 1, 2012, I leave to visit Lake Lure, Black Mountain, and Asheville N.C., after staying in two hotels along the way. And then I hopscotch from hotel to hotel, mainly Marriott suites gained through the generosity of Rebecca's job perks discount (that allows short stays at decent hotels for less than it normally costs to live), while considering the best place to secure more permanent housing before fulfilling my soul's ultimate growth purpose, of reaching as many people as possible via the gift of multidimensionality.

Later in November 2012 while in a secure, rented Lake Lure, N.C., log cabin, more precognitive—an aspect of clairvoyance—dreams occur, of tapping into a higher frequency where life is much different than the current one lived in seclusion.

Voices jostle me awake while still floating between dimensions, but I remind myself there's no man and woman conversing here in this remote log cabin among tall pines. Memory of a dream, teaching and being with James, soon surfaces while completing the usual dream recall process.

Servers placed dinners of chicken, vegetables and wild rice upon green cloths in a large elegant hall outside of many rooms. I sat to enjoy mine alone at a small mahogany table outside Room 19 before proceeding to an area where lightworkers meet. Many others soon gathered around me while sitting in a big, brown, leather armchair (Several years later I am, in this life, sitting in such a chair sharing at Florida's Miami-Deerfield Beach Theosophical Society). *One woman notes she read my book and thanks me for writing it.* (Now having published several books I have also received thanks from readers.)

We're here to share but I seem to be sharing the most. As we discuss what's happening around the world, I ask for thoughts before verifying that we are now moving through a purging and cleansing process as with the nor'easter that unexpectedly hit our Northeast coast. Humanity moves though this process to learn what we are not. Florida, I note, has already been though the process but Ohio is to experience something. (Days later the weather channel shows a huge storm beginning to move through Ohio.)

We discuss the importance of just existing in the "Black Void" before I note, 'The more people who think of one thing serve to bring it into reality sooner as thoughts manifest.' Most

96

lightworkers are very happy to talk and agree, but one does not. She starts to walk away but remains as I begin to note how my awareness changed upon Daniel's passing and continues to increase.

"But," I say, planning to continue by noting that we're unique parts of All That Is, "my bottom line is, all here is illusion."

The woman does not agree and someone then leads us to take a break. Another woman wants to walk with me as everyone flows outside but I tell her I must use the restroom. She says she'll wait for me. I move back to the hall and see a cart sitting outside Room 19. A note on vanilla-colored paper and a free beer for James sits on the cart.

Inside Room 19, James sits at a small wooden table, writing in the middle of the scantily furnished space. He looks up as I enter to tell him about the beer and note there's something along with it to sign, before asking if he dreams about me. I then note that we still live together in another realm and that's the reason we have these dreams.

Sleeping has been easier and I've awakened much less than ever before, perhaps four times in a nine-hour period instead of the every fifteen-minute intervals of years ago. Each time upon waking, glimmers of being on other realms or consciously expanding the Light within surface. The last time I woke dream recall caused me to bring forth teachings on other realms. Very much aware that I teach on other realms, I'm also now aware that bringing those teachings to this realm is indeed within the realm of possibility.

Now, in addition to sharing in-person and on-line, many recalled dream accounts are documented in books such as "Radiating Light" (*Book Of One :-) Volume 2*), to assist humanity in seeing beyond the veil of illusion that holds many people back.

PART THREE

Departed Loved
Ones Speak

Reaching Loved Ones Via The Astral Realm

Although connecting with loved ones may seem hopeless, due to various earth issues, it is possible to reach loved ones via the astral realm when you are both vibrating at the same frequency or your souls have contracted to do so at certain times. Below are some accounts of astral realm connections made before I decided to focus consciousness on higher frequencies.

Conscious astral activities started with a hospitalized departing grandmother bidding my sisters and me goodbye on October 7th 1963, while she stood before us in ethereal form in our upstairs attic bedroom. As an adult, they continued with the practice of mental telepathy between both my children and evolved to psychically hearing departed family and friends wishing to guide and inform, or relay messages to others.

In addition to many, many adventures with my departed son (named Daniel in the Lightworker's Log Book Series), within days of Daniel's passing I began to hear him, and we were able to converse in much the same way as if he stood before me in physical form. One of the first things he told me was at that time totally unbelievable: **"Mom, I never was and never will be."** So, for many days turning into months the same thought entered my brain until I finally recognized the truth of this message. Following what seemed to be his guidance I began "Science of Mind" classes, moving on to join other groups and finally landing or should I say soaring as a member of the Theosophical Society.

Another enlightening message, below and documented in my second book, came five years after his tragic motorcycle accident.

"I turn my old laptop on, ready to work on the book, but the screen begins to flash just as I open the file. I ask to hear the message. Daniel's words come quickly. He tells me once again that he never was and never will be.

"Don't you remember Mom?" he asks. "I am a part of you that came to remind you of your unlimited potential. Everything is a part of you. That's the nature of God, unlimited in all that is good. The more you create, the greater God becomes, so create more and more. Don't limit your thought of creation for there is so much more you can be and do. Let it come and stay in the flow of God's wisdom. Let it guide you and continue to protect you as we all grow nearer to God's bosom."

The computer screen continues to flash as I type his words. I just keep typing knowing typing errors can be corrected later. Daniel's essence leaves when my emotions begin to peak. The computer screen goes black as I wonder what to do next."

Seventeen years later upon reading an occult book (occult merely means unseen world) I came upon a phrase that floored me because it was one of many, many things I know now to be true, things that came to me without any teachings or readings of books. Find the phrase in *The DIALOGUES of G. de Purucker, Conversations between Teacher and Students on Genuine Theosophical Occultism*, VOLUME 1:

"So a human being comes to Earth, is born a child, lives his life, makes his gestures, has his aspirations, his hopes and his hates, and so forth, and finally disappears and we say he is 'dead.' Do you suppose that man began when he was born and ends when he dies? That is contrary to all our teaching. As a Monadic Essence he never had a beginning and never will have an end; and the elemental in its evolutionary stage called a thought, follows the same rule...."

How perfect is that to get confirmation, although none was needed, of something that seemed to come from a dead son seventeen years ago?

Soul Contracts

Planning to say a few more prayers, I switch the CD player from track six to the next track. Track seven plays for a few seconds before abruptly switching to the next track. The CD player then plays a few seconds of each subsequent song to alert me that the frequency of my last born son is with me. Ecstatic, I thank him for coming.

"It's been a while since you were here."

"You've got to forget about me."

"I thought I had, it's only for the book that I am remembering you."

"The book's not about me mom. The book is important and it will be published. Keep it simple. Don't embellish. The book is meant to let people know we are here (departed loved ones energy, always available to consult with)."

I ponder his meaning.

"I have to go now Mom."

"Wait, don't go."

A loud clap of thunder fills the air and Princess, my daughter's beloved scared terrier, jumps on me, panting heavily as her tongue hangs down in my face, like Wylie E. Coyote from the cartoon series. Knowing it's definitely time to get up, I pull back the covers, and with her in close pursuit move into the bathroom to turn on the light. Knowing her fear of lightening and propensity to claw, I note it will be alright as she sits shaking on the rug while I close the door behind me. Since the shower curtain is closed, lightening strikes are not as noticeable as in other parts of the house. Quickly, I grab a Karen Drucker CD, put it into the boom box in the living room, and turn it up loud with the speakers on the floor so Princess will hear music instead of the storm.

Efforts to control water damage from leaking walls and ceilings seem useless. After placing containers under drips, I sit on the couch to eat breakfast as Karen Drucker sings *There is No Spot Where God is Not*. Although this physical situation reminds me of the movie "The Pursuit of HappyNess," I'm thankful that at least I'm not living on the streets like the movie's main character. It's comforting to know God is everywhere in everything.

While eating and singing along to the CD, in my mind to keep positive, I realize that it's not as difficult to do as it used to be, and that alone is cause for celebration.

I begin to type thoughts down after breakfast while sitting in the living room away from leaks. At one point as Karen sings *Receiving Chant* the CD begins to skip, as if being played on a record player. "It is mine; it is mine, mine, mine. It is mine."

I close my eyes to receive the message and soon connect with my departed father-in-law's frequency.

"Don't worry about the house anymore. You've done a good job. Your part is over now".

I thank him for telling me and the now silent CD skips again.

"It is mine, mine, mine."

How grateful I am to know the soul pact we made before our birth is complete on my part! As I begin to type again, it occurs to me that people might not believe what just happened upon reading the account so I decide to test the CD by putting it into my personal CD player, which is in the bedroom. The CD plays through without a flaw.

After returning to the living room, I place it in the boom box again, and this time as the song begins to play it seems to skim through the song.

"Don't question, even for the purpose of the book. It's not necessary. Those that believe will know the truth. You've got to let the house go. Do you understand?"

"Yes."

The song now plays normally and I know it's time to stop questioning. I now remember a wonderful state of grace in late 2004, and much of 2005, where, at one point, during a loud 'discussion' about divorce with my husband, words popped out that I did not seem to have any control over. I told him I'd made a deal with his father before we were born and because he had killed me in a previous life, his father was now "setting it right." He agreed to have a son, who would be perfect to help me complete my soul's work, and after his parents died I would share in the proceeds of their estate. My husband was livid.

"You're crazy," he said with a smirk, flaring nostrils, and angry brown eyes.

I remained firm in my beliefs, despite his skepticism, and told him if he didn't divorce me then I would share in his parent's estate. And now years after our divorce I see that the settlement helped me to do exactly what I'm doing today, my soul's mission.

Ask, And Ye Shall Receive

During a very rough time, while moving through my unwanted but necessary third divorce, I silently called out for assurance that all would be well. "Please, please, I'll listen to anyone. Where are my guides, my angels, my messengers, my runners?" Deciding that my meditation time was not to be fruitful, I started to listen to a prayer on the next CD track.

The track started to play but quickly switched to the next track. Now listening to a few seconds of each track, as the CD acted erratically, I thanked the spirit of my son for coming. It surprised me that his energy returned so soon after our last communication. Anxiously, I asked him to give my mind some sort of relief. "When will I be able to start my new life?"

"You already have mom."

"He is still struggling with this divorce. It's not just about you, you know."

In the few minutes of our time together he told me again to have patience, to have faith. "But I have to admit I am living in limitation," I said as eyes filled with tears. "I know God doesn't want me to live in limitation."

"Don't forget you are not a human. It's all part of the plan. You knew before you came here that trials and tribulations were part of the plan."

107

"I have to do something. Should I call to ask him about the insurance?"

"Do what you want Mom but he doesn't need any prompting."

"Should I investigate cheaper senior areas to look at places for rent?"

"You will get your own place but it won't be where you think."

"I want my own house, something with my own fresh, clean air to breathe."

"There are more important things to remember now. Continue to act out of love. Have Faith in God. Have Faith in our Father. Remember you are a spirit and not a human."

And then he was gone as the familiar sound of cooing pigeons filled the air.

Wendy's First Message

𝔄 journal entry from January 4, 2016 notes the first message from a beloved soul, my daughter, who departed the month before, not quite twelve years after her brother. The account is documented in *After Death Communications...WOW!*

The unspeakable has happened and I do not want to go over the course of events. Suffice it to say there are no more children in my life. I feel truly alone. My beautiful, altruistic, psychically and otherwise gifted, well-educated and multi-talented daughter took her own life, believing if she stayed she would be a burden on family. God, I do not know how I shall carry on without her. And yet, since taking her own life on 12/4/15 with pills from the Michigan based Kerveocian Society and her departed brother's favorite whiskey, in a quaint Oceanside hotel, a mere mile or so from my current housing situation (the address of which was unknown to her), she now speaks.

Mom, it really doesn't matter what you do with your life from here on out. Just try to have a good time and take care of yourself. You did your bit, your contract, very well with both of us. We are eternally grateful to you for giving us the experiences we chose to have. You were a good mother, a kind and caring mother. I know you don't think this is truth, well not all of the time, but you were. We are with you now and ask you to be kind to yourself, take time for yourself, don't sweat the small stuff, as Dean always said, it's all small stuff.

It really doesn't matter if what I thought was true. You know that. You know this world is built with emotion and thought but it is changing quickly with each emotion and thought. So don't close yourself off like you did with Dean but allow yourself to expand to the fullest fun and BEingness that you can.

I hear you asking, "How can I do this with no one in my life, except one friend?" Mom, your life is empty for a reason, to be filled with greater opportunities on all fronts. To be filled with more prosperity, more love, more friends of like-mind, and more service than you can possibly imagine. Yes, continue to stay in and recognize the flow of synchronicities, and listen to us when we reach out to you. You could have made a great connection the other day but let your old self get in the way. Remember; do not act as you did after Dean passed. Let go of your beliefs and do things differently. I hear you. I know you have been doing things differently and we applaud you, but you are correct in your thinking, this change of thought, this moulding of beliefs, was a choice made before you incarnated into human form.

We are not leaving you; we are only in another form, as you know, of energy. So pay attention to the flow and step into it. Pay attention to what seems to reach out, or not reach out to you. And connect with those that reach out. That is the best advice we can offer at this time. We love you Mom.

And I am sorry, but I will not apologize for taking my own life. It is the best gift I could have given to my self, and family, and friends. Do not mourn long Mom; you have work to do.

WOW out!

Heartfelt condolences to all who have experienced the physical loss of someone they love. Know we are spirit in human form here to experience and express. There is no right or wrong only the quest to learn and practice unconditional Love.

Mother's Day Bonanzas

Mother's Day, for several years after my son's transition, always held happy surprises from the first one without him, where I was guided to a hidden computer note on the desktop computer, to the second year, where another previously unknown message popped up on my laptop, to the unexpected reminder of his loving energy cheering me up again, which is noted below.

Sometimes we act as one another's angels so it's always a good idea to interact with people to increase opportunities for what seems as miracles to happen, always when least expected. Thinking the day's excursion was meant to inform myself about a second trip to the spiritual Big Sky Retreat, I rose earlier than usual to support the event with my meeting attendance. The usual classroom held perhaps twenty people of various ages, many of them known to me from our last fun-filled excursion through Idaho, Wyoming and Montana. I sat down at a table with Ann who had gone early with our group last year for the longer road trip that included days in Yellowstone.

Today video equipment didn't seem to be working so meeting attendees filed into the much larger sanctuary with working audio/visuals. Taking a seat in the back I was surprised to see our video from last year's Big Sky group on the huge screen. Ann came into the sanctuary, remarked on the video, and soon persuaded me to sit up front with her saying we'd see it better; even though I told her I'd seen it at least fifty times, since I was the one that made it.

I followed her as she walked down the aisle of the second row but something made me sit in the aisle behind her. My attention was drawn to the plaque on the back of a chair to my right. It read, "I am the Divine Light :-) In Loving Memory of (my son's full name—deleted here for privacy purposes)." Stunned, with tear-filled eyes, I thanked Ann for leading me to the plaque paid for so many months ago; I had no idea where it was. DAD's loving energy reminded me yet again, yes, Spirit works thorough everyone. What a Happy Mother's Day gift from that spirit of my last born son!

And then there's the first Mother's Day, where now childless, both adult departed kids appeared in my mind's eye, while driving to the Miami/Deerfield Beach Theosophical Society. As a catchy tune played on the car radio, I saw them, arm in arm, laughing along and mimicking the words, pointing at me in jest. They were, in effect, saying, "Na ne, na ne, boo boo, we are out of the game and you are not!"

The song playing was about how while babies we listened to our Momma sing to us, without a care in the world, and it resonated strongly, for memories of singing "You Are My Sunshine," with them as infants cradled in loving arms arose as a rainbow filled sunrise. But now, the song noted, all grown up we had to "work for the money."

As their images continued to grace my mind, I too laughed and sang along; not giving a hoot about what other drivers might see and hear!

Tears flow as I type this but I remind myself this is just a dream. This is just a dream world where I have programmed these kinds of things in to keep me inspired and stay on track.

The Red Light

Although now accustomed to anomalies, every once in a while a new one surprises me; this one came at 3:14 AM, as I tried to figure out what woke me after finally falling asleep thirty-minutes earlier. The nightstand to my right held a large black telephone, recently purchased, and for the first time a red light shone in the darkness.

Still groggy with sleep, I reached over and touched the red light, which turned out to be some kind of button on the telephone. The light went away but quickly came back on again with a small noise! I turned it off again. It came on again with a small noise and once again I turned it off now beginning to be fearful of an unknown abnormality. Yet, something in me said, "No. I know, someone is just letting me know they're here."

"Thank you," I then said out loud, "for letting me know that you're here, that you're with me. I appreciate it."

How amazing it is that even after what appears to be physical death loved ones can alert us of their presence by triggering electronics!

Hearing no message, I then fell promptly back asleep.

PART FOUR

Multidimensional Living

The Multidimensional HU-man

𝕱requency is a malleable element of consciousness. For those unaware, as Nikola Tesla noted so long ago, EVERYTHING is a matter of frequency and vibration. Our very bodies consist of billions, and billions, of life-atoms oscillating at various frequencies, and some of us, as noted in this book, have the ability to raise those frequencies to reveal more of our constitution through what can be referred to as 'astral sight,' or less frequently experienced 'mental sight,' tapping into yet another realm of our constitution.

Frequency determines our ability to experience and express differently, increasing opportunities with each change in the body's vibrational rate. Frequencies referred to as lower or 'negative' such as confusion, judgment, and fear keep us in matching lower states of awareness and vibration, limiting perception. Clearly, if one desires to tap into clairvoyant states and go beyond those states of awareness then one must take steps to do so. Eliminating synthetic substances in or on the body was my first step, followed by changes in dietary habits, meditation, and study enabling the flow of wisdom to occur upon reaching frequencies of what many refer to as the Higher Self/Reincarnating Ego, Human Monad, and at peak times Spiritual Monad.

The frequency of a multidimensional HU-man changes at will of the host within physical form and determines the state of one's consciousness, whether one is tapping into those frequencies of what may be referred to as intuition or of clairvoyance. *Intuition, a clear knowing without physical evidence*, as theosophist Alice A. Bailey notes in *Serving Humanity*, is a "growth primarily in sensitivity and in an inner response to the soul." It is "an expression of the Buddhic principle", and fully unfolded a different frequency than that of clairvoyance, "beyond the world of ego and of form." The frequency of clairvoyance, as described in my accounts, carries many different wavelengths of sound and sight leading one on an ever-present roller coaster ride of differentiation in objects within space and time.

And, as noted by G. de Purucker in the second of a series of books, *II THE ESOTERIC OR ORIENTAL SCHOOL: STEPS IN THE INITIATORY CYCLE*:

"**Spiritual clairvoyance** is the faculty of vision, of seeing, with the inner eye; and it is not so much a seeing of forms and of things, as a getting of knowledge, and because this getting of knowledge comes in a way which has a close parallel to seeing with the physical eye, it is called spiritual 'clairvoyance'- direct vision."

It is only through the raising of what seems as the body's vibratory rate that one can easily tap into those higher states of intuition and clairvoyance.

Again, within the matrix of illusion in which we seem to exist, our world of frequency and vibration constantly changes with every reaction, emotion, thought, word, and deed. So-called hidden planes within our reality begin to reveal themselves as our body frequency increases and we open our mind to accept different beliefs and experiences.

In order of materiality, as noted by C.W. Leadbeater in *The Astral Plane* (first published in 1895), from denser to finer they are the **physical, astral, devachanic (mental), sushuptic (dreamless sleep), nirvanic and two much higher planes** that are far above the range of most people's conception.

Further adding to our experience and expression as spirits taking on souls, each of these planes of consciousness have sub-planes, which also have sub-planes, so our reality continues to change not only with each body our soul takes on, but also merging finally and wholly with our spirit, beyond the life of our soul, continuing to uniquely experience and express in never ending cycles. Those seeking in-depth information on this and other esoteric subjects may consider the teachings of Theosophy, a mind child of Helena Petrovna Blavatsky that continues, as we HU-mans, to unfold in ever-richer states.

In 2006 I became very much aware of this truth: as humans evolving in a 3D state of awareness/consciousness: our body frequency continually rises IF not tampered with synthetically. EVERYTHING affects the body's frequency and therefore health and the ability to use our intuition and to tap into unseen realms. After monitoring and eliminating anything detrimental put in or on my body, my personal awakening began as the body's frequency consistently rose. (See my first three books for details of Western 'medical' experiences and how I left them behind).

As body frequency rises and we develop our intuitive capacity, telepathic impressions come more rapidly from all forms of life. Of course, accurate impression may be altered based on our 'filters' of experience and expression. At first we may seem to hear plant life and/or animals speaking before developing the capacity to become in tune with people and then move on to higher frequencies, until, while still in human form, we easily tap into our Higher Ego and, for very few of us, our Spiritual Monad.

Working along the lines of mental telepathy is very different than working along the lines of spiritual telepathy. The level of ones consciousness determines the impressions received. For instance some people, such as mediums, are more prone to receive impressions from astral or etheric frequencies rather than those of the higher mental plane. Impressions from mental levels, which are, Bailey relates, concrete, abstract or of a more exalted nature make their impress upon the minds of those who have attained a true measure of focus upon the mental plane. Again, correct interpretation is key; the energy source must be known and stated clearly, whether it is the mind, astral body, energy body, or brain. Impressions must originate from mental levels to the brain, avoiding astral energies to be devoid of error and not affected with emotion.

Contacts emanating from higher sources may be mixed with lower egotic impressions until the ability to discern is honed and ones body frequency rises. Sensitivity to telepathic impressions can be questionable when coming from unknown sources. For instance, I once believed, for days, that neighbors were holding a hostage in their home, until finally, full of gusto and compassion to assist, after entering their backyard and looking through glass doors attempting to confirm suspicions, finding no evidence, boldly approached the neighbors after they returned from work; their puppy was upset every time he had to be locked in a cage to stop him from messing up the house while his masters worked. Relief came upon learning pleas heard telepathically, to be released from bondage, were from a dog.

As related by Bailey in *Telepathy and the Etheric Vehicle*, developing telepathic sensitivity is a normal unfoldment of innate ability (our evolution) not a forced process. As one "acquires true freedom of thought, and the power to be receptive to the impression of the abstract mind, he creates for himself a reservoir of thought which becomes available at need for the helping of other people, and for the necessities of his growing world service."

Evolution in my mind means waking up to the real 'world' and it unfolds as two very separate states. In the *first awakening state*, as our frequency rises beyond the usual condition and conditioning, intuition increases making us able to intuitively know when something may not be right; we may then investigate to confirm our newly awakened sense, taking steps to right what we perceive as wrongs, or avoid manipulation by power seeking individuals. Or else we may find it easier to merely remain within our usual circumstances, which eventually change to assure action on our part even if that action results in physically leaving the planet, making it possible for the soul to evolve in another life form. Personally, I have found it very beneficial to continue to raise my frequency and now view life on earth in multiple ways thereby avoiding undue harm to my physical HU-man Host.

The higher our vibrational rate the more able we are to discern, by using our very own Higher Self as a guide. As a soul we chose to experience and express certain things, and many of us are now balancing all experiences and expressions as we recall, unfold, or bring in, so to speak, other aspects hidden within us – those multidimensional experiences and expressions usually left unacknowledged. When the frequency of our body first rises we begin to tap into what many refer to as the Fourth Dimension (4D), another place in our consciousness consisting of, as our 3D world, various frequencies. Veils of illusion continue to thin so it is becoming easier to tap into this emotional astral realm. This dimension is a frequency of space where departed souls may roam; we may communicate with guides, be informed, OR misled, and more.

Clairvoyance and clairaudience are two of many natural abilities most of us have forgotten how to use. Are they a blessing or a curse? As higher psychic development occurs we may find ourselves asking this question. Tapping into higher states of consciousness, particularly in a 4D state of awareness, is rather risky due to various characteristics, so one must achieve and maintain a higher vibrational rate to avoid attracting what may be referred to as 'negative, non-helpful influences'. 4D is a reflection of 3D, an emotional field of consciousness where things are subjective and open to the awareness of individual, ego-based consciousness. 5D is a different state of awareness where things are objective, all-inclusive, non-emotional and geared in We Consciousness or Oneness. Based on Buddhist teachings, nearly everything we experience, whether in dream states or seeming awake is Sludge, ever-changing consciousness, including all soul experience. It is very rare, impossible for most of us, to tap into Pure Being, which is devoid of consciousness, the Eternal Potential. The best we can achieve at this point in time is to operate from Creator Consciousness.

One must always use resonance focusing on the heart and discernment using the mind when living as a multidimensional HU-man.

Those tapping into what is thought of as the 4D realm can receive information from 4D aspects of consciousness. And yet, knowing the nature of 4D we must each follow our own truth, while maintaining a high vibrational rate to avoid manipulation.

As noted in *Wisdom of the Mystic Masters* by Joseph J. Weed when our solar plexus center awakens the lower psychic faculties we become aware of "beings, sights, sounds and smells which exist on the astral plane... a world whose inhabitants are no more dependable or wiser than the average man you might meet on the street, and often far more fallible."

As already mentioned, when one taps into this state of awareness we hear voices and may visibly see (as perhaps mirages or shadows), or intuitively sense, forms that are not seen by our physical senses. And when tapping into the astral world one can experience attempts to terrify or stimulate an emotional response. We may be impressed by what we see and hear but knowing the deceptive nature of 4D we must always protect ourselves from being trapped by dubious information.

During the *second state of waking-up* we fine tune our intuition to the point where no physical or 4D investigation is necessary. Now we just KNOW and can more easily tap into higher frequencies of awareness such as 5D and above. These are realms that envelop everything and everyone as One, all here playing a game on earth while each expressing and experiencing uniquely; but in the meantime, our Overself/Spiritual Monad remains unaffected.

For the purpose of this book, *Multidimensional Living: Moving Beyond Astral Adventures*, I shall note that the majority of experiences herein described occurred mainly during my first stage of waking up. And since heightened senses and frequencies made them possible I refer to them as astral, being possible to occur beyond the usual physical experience. The experiences noted below occurred as I continued to raise the body's frequency, allowing for glimpses beyond the astral realm.

Remember, everything we hear, even the inner voices that speak to us, comes from our own selves, our union with Omniscience (Consciousness that incubates creation), which may appear as other entities, guides from another dimension, or even angels. *And yet, we truly are spirits in human form having a physical experience, but it is now time to experience and express in greater ways. We have experienced life in human form many times and must now realize that what happens here on earth is an illusion of our own making. It is time to be the HU-mans we came to experience and express!*

Early Multidimensional Experiences

This excerpt from *Lightworker's Log: Transformation* documents how we can interact with higher realms to raise our frequency.

I was back home an hour later and soon in bed, sporadically rising every fifty or ninety minutes, each time recalling a glimmer of something, but unable to recall what it was. Exhausted at dawn, I rose again, and this time, remembered.

A voice told me I was getting more power.

As I lie still to receive it, I felt the familiar heat spreading from my heart's center throughout the body. The heat became almost unbearable. This time I did not throw off the bedcovers, but remained still, reminding myself that's what I'd done so many times in 2006 and 2007. I laid there feeling my entire body vibrating as if plugged into a light socket. I have felt this energy before but not, to my recollection, to this extent. And when I thought I could not stand it any longer, it seemed to be over.

I opened my eyes and raised my head slowly still feeling a counterclockwise rotation of energy circulating directly above my head. Again, it's now a familiar feeling, but not to this extent. This strong beam of energy came undoubtedly from Source, the Universal Cosmic Energy that will help to bring me Home again.

Gratefulness overwhelmed me as I thanked God for the experience and for carrying me through it. My brain began to kick into gear but could not deny what occurred. Failing miserably, it tried to convince me the communication was not from Source. But I now know how Source works. It never demands but guides by communicating certain things. It is always my choice to follow up on the communication or not.

Spirit Guides

One sunny morning in March 2008, I woke as usual to listen to a daily mediation and prayer CD, but was guided to the holosync track, which I put on repeat to hear again, and again. An odd thing seemed to happen after a short time not knowing if I was asleep or awake. In addition to the sound of rain falling, and other musical notes, there were voices and other noises not usually heard. As I listened with eyes closed, I began to feel very peaceful with a sense of my arms rising simultaneously, up off the bed. After both arms were about a foot off the bed my body rose as well! It seemed very real and exciting as I felt my body being lifted towards the sky.

I then sensed someone at the door, and, in my mind, was at the door instantly. The door opened slightly and there stood a little girl. I was upset with her for interrupting me and asked her what she wanted, wanting her to go away so I could continue my meditation, but then I realized she was one of my guides. Next to her sat a small boy with an olive colored complexion, dark hair, and a turban like headdress on his head. They began to speak.

I opened my eyes remembering, "There are four more years of work to do. You were introduced to your two main guides today. Remember them. They are always with you. Now go in peace."

What a shock it was to discover that the holosync track had played for more than an hour upon carefully rising to look at my watch! Now fueled with excitement, I grabbed my bedside writing pad and ink pen to document everything, and then decided to type it into the computer too.

Accomplished Soul Contract

Furniture becomes a necessity upon moving into my very own space at the ripe age of 58-years-old. Finally, it's time to live alone, yet, ads for the desired leather couch and chair seem priced way too high so I'm guided to look in local newspapers for used belongings. It seems reasonable to look at an "almost new" leather living room set, for a mere $60, two-miles from my newly rented eight-room house.

Minutes after speaking with a woman, who sounds very eager to sell her furniture and move to California, I arrive at a brown-colored house sitting on a quiet cul de sac, which looks empty from the outside. When the front mahogany door opens, emptiness of the air inside, appearing devoid of vibrant energy so apparent in my own place, causes me to step back before acknowledging it's owner. Ruth's small, pretty face is featured by long, dull looking red hair and large blues eyes, looking almost too large. As she welcomes me into the extremely dark space, filled with the smell of cigarette smoke, I remark on the lack of light.

"My boyfriend likes it like that," Ruth says.

I stop walking, ask her to turn on a light, and then notice the only light there to turn on is the one in the hall. At this point I've already decided that my task is not to buy furniture. Why am I here?

With an eager look on her thin, now tired-looking face, Ruth waves her hand into the living room where a large, off-white leather lounger and chair sit. I focus on the furniture rather than looking more around what seems as a depressing, sparsely furnished space. It looks worth $60, but not to me as it's permeated with the strong scent of cigarette smoke, and, sadly, a sense of negativity. With a knowing look, I calmly announce that sometimes I think I'm going to a place for one thing and soon learn I really go there for something else.

"This," I say looking into her pretty blue eyes, "is one of those times."

Ruth nervously looks toward the rear of the house while recalling how she heard her dead sister talk to her when she was 17-years-old. She does not look much older than that as I determine that now she needs to know about the veil between us and our departed loved ones, how it collapses for those willing to listen.

Someone stirring in another room of the house catches my attention as I begin to tell Ruth about the veil being thinner. She perks up, listens intently, and within seconds a small man with a silver and black mustache moves quickly out of what I figure to be their bedroom. With brown, dirty-looking short hair, he looks like he just crawled out of bed, sticks out his unusually small right hand and says, "Glad to meet you."

I ask for his name and am surprised to hear my second husband's name. "You must think I sound crazy, huh David?"

He nods a non-convincing no, and with a cagey look, moves into the adjoining room to sit in a small task chair in front of a laptop computer. I quickly finish telling Ruth part of what I'm sent to say but can't say more, for I know David is listening just as intently, if not more so. "I'll think about the furniture," I announce before turning toward the front door.

Ruth takes the hint and follows me out to my car. Sensing David's state of mind, I tell her about the Christian who helped edit my book draft, when the process started months ago, but now will not help because he thinks it is evil; peppered with many communications from, and adventures with, my departed son. Ruth and I now talk about religion. She has always been more spiritual, not believing what was taught by her parents.

"We are One," I announce, smiling broadly. "There is no separation."

She acknowledges that she knew it all along. Now, I know it's time to say the rest of what I've been sent to say.

"Your time with David is over."

"I know. He got a job in California and wants me to go with him but he's too controlling. I just want to leave now instead of at the end of the month, but don't want to leave all my things behind just to get out of the relationship."

"I've left everything in the past and you can too, especially if you are still financially supporting him. Sometimes it's just not worth the cost of staying."

Ruth looks down at the driveway as I continue to tell her more about my soon to be published first book, which describes, as in the *Celestine Prophecy*, how people steal energy from other people. She nods sadly to let me know, yes, for the past twenty years; David has and continues to feed off of her energy, leaving her exhausted whenever he's around. With a flash, I realize, since she is probably not menstruating anymore David will soon find a younger, more energetic host to steal from, leaving her alone and out of her element if she chooses to move with him.

She gladly takes the book I offer, which happens to be in my car, as I note, "This author's first book is titled *Codependency No More* and I highly recommended it. I read it myself many years ago."

Ruth jabs her left forefinger into the middle of her right palm and twists it vigorously back and forth.

"That hits it on the head."

She'll surely get the book.

"We'll talk again."

"I'm really busy and I've already said what I came to say. Now it's up to you to open your mind more."

Before getting into my car I give her some tips to stay away from David as much as she can.

"It's best to focus on your inner core," I say calmly pointing to the middle of my chest. "That's the Light of God in there and we all have it."

"I've always felt that," she says with a broad smile.

Before closing my car door to drive away my last message flows. "Get outside on the grass as much as you can and concentrate on bringing the Light of God down within you."

And that's what it's like to connect with the "God Network," to tap into our god-given sixth sense. We are one another's angels with messages to share in the so-called journey of awakening, and sharing them helps us as much as it does the receiver.

Family Connections Via The Astral Realm

𝕯aily journaling continues but something tells me that this year's entire adventures will not be in a published book. One sunny day upon returning from my usual walk around the carefully manicured senior neighborhood, to radiate light in the area, I return to see a text message on the small, red flip-phone in my pocket. Surprised to see it since I hadn't heard the phone make any kind of noise, I happily notice it's from my daughter-in-law who rarely contacts me, asking if, at my granddaughter's request, I can come and stay during spring break. "I'll call you tonight," it said.

Yes, I think, since my daughter-in-law now works full-time she needs someone to care for Abigail—my granddaughter's name in books—during her time away. Knowing this is an opportunity to reconnect with them, meet soul contracts, and that Abigail, even from birth being much more evolved than any of us, and still so at this point, knows what she is doing; living a very different, quiet and uncluttered life I must consider my response. Yet, I know everything will be alright so I text back an affirmative reply. My daughter-in-law doesn't phone later to discuss plans.

Abigail's hearty energy comes to me, in mind, as I'm drifting off to sleep after midnight; she's not sure if I'll be spending the week at their house because "Mommy is still thinking about it." We talk while on the astral plane and soon I note the Divine Plan is in order, things will happen accordingly; and after professing our love for one another, her energy dissipates upon noting she is tired and has to sleep. I too fall asleep happy to have connected with Abigail. It's been a long time since her dad transitioned out of this physical realm, but quickly returned, in wee hours of the night, to take me through astral realms so we could hold her, and sing to her, and comfort her. How wonderful to be in touch with Abigail on the astral realm again, especially since physical world connections are few and far between.

And yes, upon returning from the "Gary Renard Happy Dream Cruise" I did spend time with Abigail, who sought advice on spirit orbs, and my daughter-in-law who requested a house blessing. I cleansed the 11-room house with large back porch and garage thoroughly, double checked it when done and did my best to fill their house with Love and Light, and to let them both know they are loved beyond all measure. Gratitude filled me upon returning to a quiet, uncluttered home, leaving behind the hectic, weary life of a single mom that I know only so very well.

Upon returning, I agreed to attend the April 4th (exactly five years from the date of my son's transition) funeral service of a friend who lost her son; it was something I had to do to close the circle since I did not attend my own son's service. And what a lovely fifth dimensional service it was speaking of graduation and completed soul plans! Now I consider the service as my son's for it left strong impressions of changing into a new form, a new form that physical human eyes cannot see, and yet is still there on a different frequency going on to yet another level of consciousness.

Anchoring Energy

New energies continue to bombard us here on earth. Many of us anchor that energy just by being where we are. We always, even unknowingly, transmute denser energies into the higher vibration of Love by our presence. Several years of anchoring this energy into earth's grid taught me that it does make a difference.

Very intense frequencies permeate the planet during all types of earth changes, increased geomagnetic activity, planetary alignments, solar and lunar eclipses, etc. Each event changes energies around us and needs grounding to cement the new Mother Earth. Our bodies change right along with Gaia to remain on the same wavelength.

For many years, these events worried me until physical manifestation of changed consciousness happened right before my eyes during a tornado. This occurred after several years of work to change the way I thought. Knowing that thoughts physically manifest to create the world in which we live helped me to mold a peaceful existence despite surrounding physical circumstances.

A sudden gust of strong wind prompted me to stop writing and rise from the big, brown, Lazy Boy chair to investigate one sunny 2011 day in late spring. Sounds of debris hitting solid objects resounded through the air as I walked toward the back porch. They reminded me of hurricane sounds but it was not that season so I remained unafraid.

Peace filled me even when I opened the back screen door to investigate. There, before my eyes to the right, sat a funnel cloud. Instead of cowering in fear with recognition my attention drew to a variety of objects that seemingly floated in mid-air. Pieces of wood, roof tiles, stones and other small objects swirled in the funnel as I watched in wonder. It didn't occur to me that I stood a mere twenty-foot distance away from a tornado as I stood with gaping mouth watching the scene.

It was so awesome that all I wanted to do was record the event so, of course, I closed my mouth and ran back into the house to get a camcorder. The funnel moved past my rented home and down the canal by the time I returned. Tiles ripped off several houses a mile away as I watched trying to video the scene in vain. And very soon, the funnel disappeared.

I reentered the house to finish the day's work but rose again hungry two hours later. Several people had strolled past the house, which was very unusual for the very quiet neighborhood. More people stood near the drive as I backed out for a quick drive to buy fresh vegetables.

Police tape and a scene from the movies sat around the corner five houses away. Maneuvering around a crowd of gaping neighbors, I headed around the tape. A quick glance to my left revealed several damaged roofs, scattered debris and ripped up lawns. The scene played out throughout the neighborhood as I made my way, sometimes driving on people's lawns, to get to the store (Yes, fresh salad is now a must!).

The telephone rang insistently as I entered the house upon returning home. "Are you alright?" my sister inquired, quickly explaining that my neighborhood, and two others, was now featured on national news, for the freak tornado that ran amuck came out of nowhere.

All I could do was shake my head in wonder as I laughingly explained how the funnel cloud entertained me for several minutes. My sister could not comprehend the state of consciousness that kept me safe. No, I was crazy for not cowering in the closet upon seeing the funnel.

This illustrates a very important point for those holding the Light and anchoring new energies. We are safe in the bosom of Mother Earth despite the consciousness of others seemingly apart from us. It makes no difference where we live for when we hold the Light with true Oneness consciousness no threat disarms that state of awareness.

Continue to radiate and spread Light, for that is what you are!

Note: Anchoring Energy is a *Bits of Wisdom* book excerpt.

Momma's Goodbye

Sometimes when we are in the midst of drama we do not always look for the gifts or be aware of the importance of soul plans, which many may note as synchronistic events. But if we are tapped into our Higher Self we can assist with not only our own soul's evolution but help others do the same, as noted in this account of my mother's transition. The sequence of events is hard to recall but I know a physical body is not who we are. As a soul it seems my plan to spread the news of another way to be in what seems a physical world, so try to see beyond the drama.

Momma passed on Thursday, May 26, 2011, after a fourteen-hour drama involving the whole family. Terry, my youngest brother, who lives with Momma called me around 9:30 in the morning, the day of my grandson Samuel's high school graduation, to report with much distress that they just got to the hospital. Since I came across her "Living Will" only days before, in a place where I look at least once a month and never saw it, I knew this hospital visit was her last. Momma had vomited blood, Terry noted, twice, before he finally demanded she go to the hospital, which she had been adamantly refusing to do.

Having worked at the hospital I knew the fastest route, grabbed the Living Will and headed out the door. Less than thirty minutes later, I gave it to the ER doctor as he walked through the hall because it was clear to me that Momma was already gone. She did not appear to acknowledge me and seemed totally removed. As I now recall, she opened her eyes, maybe once or twice during a two-hour period before an inept nurse tried to stick her with the second I.V. needle. Dried blood caked on Momma's right hand and in her mouth; I did the best I could to calmly remove it, but could not get it all out of her mouth.

Momma was scratching my neck and when I put her hand down she dug a nail into her own neck; a pool of blood poured out of the site. That was when I remembered Momma had very low platelets.

My daughter came from work for a bit before driving to her next job site in Boca Raton, thirty-minutes away. She had already planned to leave work early due to Samuel's graduation banquet. This would be the family's first high school graduation the 'normal' way and we all looked forward to the celebration. She, Terry and I stayed as calm as we could but the hospital was undergoing some kind of renovation as workers were doing construction on the other side of the wall where Momma laid in a small hospital bed to fit the, I thought, too small room. I knew it bothered us more than Momma and immediately got the metaphor.

After they gave her the first bag of albumin, Momma began to have convulsions. I did not, at the time, realize why (with liver disease you need a low protein diet and this stuff is 100% protein; she was already dehydrated and had an empty stomach), so much for quality care in a hospital that held all her medical records! Blood, from her second I.V. site, soaked onto my pale yellow blouse, while I tried to stop her knee from bruising as she jerked it up to hit the bedrail, in what seemed like spasms of pain; I stood there silently pushing Light into Momma with my hands to try and ease her discomfort. Then I took a break to wash the blood off of my top.

The ER doctor confided in the hall that Momma was not going to make it and I soon explained this to my younger sister, Ruth, as she listened while working in Joplin, MO. Momma's next angel of a nurse said not to lose hope. He soon talked the doctor into giving Momma morphine after I told him she was in dire pain. They didn't want to give her anything other than Antivan, a tranquilizer, until all the labs came back. I wasn't sure they knew about all her conditions, or bothered to search her medial records, but made sure they knew she was a DNR with a Living Will. It was one of my tasks, as her legally designated medical representative, and agreed upon before our birth, I just knew it.

Ruth's life partner, Naomi, arrived with our long time friend, Sarah and shortly after my daughter arrived again and stayed for a bit before rushing home to change and get Samuel to his graduation banquet. An hour or two later, we all moved up to the I.C.U. Momma's doctor, who she saw for many years before seeing the woman doctor near Ruth and Naomi's home walked swiftly toward the I.C.U., as we sat waiting for them to get Momma settled into bed. I jumped up to let him know she was there. He said she was the reason he had came and minutes later, totally unlike his usually calm and polite self, angrily asked, "What the hell happened?" He, too, told me she would not make it. I made sure they all knew Momma was not to have any life-prolonging procedures, and at the last possible minute, left to change clothes and attend Samuel's banquet; a bold move, but I knew Momma would wait for our return.

It came as a complete surprise to see my departed son's widow, Rachel, and granddaughter, Abigail, standing outside as I walked through the school parking lot. Samuel's other grandmother and my ex-husband came as well, which made the table half-full. At exactly 9:30 p.m., when the banquet was scheduled to end, Terry texted my daughter Rebecca's phone:

"You better come now."

She showed me the phone and I left quickly after saying goodbye.

It took a mere ten minutes to make the usual thirty minute drive back to Holy Cross Hospital. I knew no one would stop me on the freeway and traffic was surprisingly clear. I ran through the ER entrance knowing if I went in the usual way the guard would delay me and it might be too late. An angel allowed me to interrupt her as she registered a new patient so I could quickly get upstairs. It sure helped to know the hospital after working there!

A nurse told me before I entered the room that it would be very soon. As Sarah stood nearby looking at the trio, Naomi held Momma's right hand while Terry held her left in the brightly lit hospital room. With a nod of her head, Naomi immediately asked if I wanted to "come over here." We changed places. And as Terry blubbered through tears about knowing what Momma wanted him to do, most likely, I knew, stop fighting with and love his older brother; I held Momma's right hand with my left one and placed my right hand upon her stomach, and then, I did my job. I poured the purest, brightest Light into Momma and helped her to move into the Light. As my physical eyes looked about the room, my mind's eyes saw her standing across from a group of etheric beings. I knew they were her soul group; energetic impressions of my departed son, Daddy, favorite aunt and uncle, and lots more grouped behind them. I watched Momma and felt her immense JOY as she flowed toward them and into the Light. Tears filled my eyes knowing I will never, ever, forget, the JOY beyond all comprehension.

When I looked up, most of the family now filled the room and I knew we were all there due to soul contracts, saying goodbye to yet another physical form that would someday *be reborn. As each member said their final goodbye before leaving the hospital room I stood back trying to compose myself. And after everyone left I again thanked Momma for staying so long in what appeared as years of difficult situations to complete her soul plan. Well done Momma!*

Weary, but happy Momma's lifetime of what seemed a never-ending struggle for survival—from shock treatments for so-called schizophrenia, multiple health conditions due to prescribed drugs, six live births and two miscarriages, to family and other issues—was complete, the trip to my car took much more time than on the way to see that final breath. A flood of tears came as I settled behind the wheel. Minutes later, I turned the key to realize the radio was playing. Tears slowed upon hearing, "She's like the wind," for I immediately picked up on yet another synchronistic event. Yes, just as my son, Momma is ecstatic to be free of human life!

What I now refer to as the essence of my last-born son told me a month or so later that Momma is transitioning very well. And during a Sacred breath Workshop weeks later on July 11th, while wondering why I was there, for it seemed geared toward helping people to do things I've already done, Momma came through loud and clear to relate the same thing. A beautiful image of her much younger face with gorgeously shining black curly hair appeared in my mind's eye as the Workshop group participated in a silent period. Momma said she would be helping the family from the Otherside and I could go forward and not worry about them; I am to continue on my path of "Light" work.

And that's what it's like to live with, as Wendy, my now departed daughter, would say, "a foot in both worlds."

Leaving the physical form is a joyous experience. Knowing the immense joy and ecstasy upon passing from our dense physical form, which is unmatched on any other realm of existence, helps us to make the transition of our eternal energy much easier. We are indeed lifted to a higher plane/frequency to continue our evolution as souls.

3D versus 5D reality

As noted in the following journey entry, personal evolution can be tracked by a conscious mind. By mid-2012, with a bit more than one-month of being 'home-free' I became aware of another progression.

Life is a matter of balance and neutrality, and apparently, I am learning both. Flying is very cumbersome and somehow seems meant to take people out of their comfort zones. Today while flying through space and time on a 737 I'm somewhat more out of the comfort zone I became accustomed to while living in hotels for the past five weeks. I really thought traveling with just a carry on backpack and small travel bag, sans the usual two suitcases packed with sufficient clothes and spring water for two weeks, would make the trip care-free. I was wrong.

To begin, instead of the preferred non-stop, only one one-stop flight looked doable to me because it offered the least amount of trip time. It still astounds me how airlines stretch a four-hour flight into twelve or even twenty hours by making people take several planes to get to destinations. Of course, I realize that in 3D reality corporations have become accustomed to

getting the most money they can; and don't get this ego started on who exactly owns the airlines.

Clearly, the events of September 11, 2001 have had much farther reaching effects than many people ever thought possible, and even now, while striving to maintain a cord to my beloved 5D reality, I'm faced with acknowledging these changes while physically dealing with them. How can you deny the 3D reality when you seem to live in it or pass through it?

On my last airline trip for an 11-11-11 event I experienced being in two worlds quite consciously when checking baggage through airport security. In one airport I stood in a long line watching a large security agent bark orders at those in front of me. People had to take their shoes off, display their computers, place medications in see-though bags, etc., and then they had to stand still in front of a new type of body scanner.

I took it all in and consciously made the decision not to stand still in front of the body scanner. Minutes later, as my turn came to face the barking security agent; he ducked his head under a table as if searching for something. I quickly took the opportunity to move into a different line and breezed through, walking only through the older mandatory x-ray scanner.

Another opportunity to stand in a very, very, long line presented itself before boarding another flight in Phoenix, AZ as I stood in line watching people join the line unconcerned that it was so long. But a few people skirted under ropes to seemingly make their own line. They were met with another, much quieter security agent who did not force them through the body scanner.

Intuition told me I too could skirt under the ropes to join them. Yet, I thought about what the people I stood among might think or do for now I stood in the middle of the now very, very, very long weaving line. Upon reaching the body scanner I asked for and was afforded the opportunity to be physically frisked by a woman security agent who apologized as she completed her task. As with other security agents, I told her she should consider other employment. She answered that she badly needed the job and the benefits it afforded and I truly understood, even though I knew her vibration level would soon no longer allow her to continue in the same job she now so expertly performed.

Another opportunity of 3D versus 5D realities presented itself several months later as I began to disembark from a cruise ship. Of course, intuition forced me to leave the ship hours earlier than ego planned. I found myself standing near the back of a long line of people taking advantage of the opportunity to disembark, earlier than everyone else with their own luggage — rather than have porters handle it so it had to be searched for in a large terminal after disembarking.

Minutes after I joined the line it began to very slowly move toward the stairs behind the group I stood with. Intuition again prompted me to move quickly. I was to turn around and join the people in the front of the line who formed new lines as they moved down the stairs. I watched them and announced to the woman next to me that we could easily join those who were now in front of the line. She said she didn't want to get her teeth bashed in.

At that point, I realized she was in the same mind set I had experienced months earlier in the airport and said goodbye. It took very little effort to quickly join the newly forming lines downstairs that led to freedom. I breezed off the ship, easily found my car in the parking garage, and made it home in half the usual time.

Today, this early morning flight got me out of bed much earlier than usual. And despite paying $514 for the airline ticket — more than I am accustomed to paying — I was unable to choose my seats upon booking but requested aisle seats noting plenty were available. Two weeks before the first flight intuition guided me to check seat assignments online. Lo and behold, I did not have an aisle seat for the first and longest flight. And now the only aisle seats available were touted as having extra leg room for $14 (they do not).

Airport security took my new tube of toothpaste as I moved though the line and my spring water as well. It's bad enough that you cannot take your own water but then to be forced to go without or purchase the single brand airlines now offer—which is merely bottled tap water—for an exceedingly high cost seems paramount to criminal. Of course, in *another state of awareness I could just purchase the chlorine and fluoride-filled tap water they pretend is better bottled, magnetize it, and be done with it. But why should I if I can taste the difference and it doesn't suit me? Why should I be forced to buy something inferior at a cost more than 400% of what I pay for something superior at home? Why should I have to give up my brand-new tube of toothpaste and have to go though the trouble of trying to purchase the same brand in another state at an increased cost? Is this not about getting people out of their comfort zone? How many people really believe that terrorists line up to threaten Americans with water and toothpaste? How many people continue to be filled with that fear?*

There are many questions on my mind now as I travel with my one small carry-on bag and backpack. Obviously, even cutting down on what I travel with has not yet put me into that free-zone where I'm unaccosted by forces seemingly outside myself. Being in the public is no fun. At least the woman who talked non-stop since the last flight began was behind me and not next to me. One can be grateful for certain things and that's the key. Remain grateful!

Clearing Dense Energies

Seeking new ways to live comes by investigating possibilities, and so from April 2012-2013, merely twelve months, I stay at twenty-six places, in five U.S. states. One stay in particular helped many facets of my diamond being to shine, while keeping soul contracts, honing clairvoyant and intuitive capabilities, opening portals, clearing dense energies, balancing karma, and claiming my power to move out of unhealthy situations. As Hanna Ehlers of Lightworkers Unite from the United Kingdom noted in one of her updates, ever so eloquently:

> *"I understood in that moment in order to release the fears and the grip of the mind you must face them and come to the end where no more can exist.*

> *"I suddenly realized what this new life was that I had taken on for myself. It hit me clear as day that I had been trying to avoid uncontrollable situations and trying to sneak my way through life, but that life was not like that and that I would from now on have to face a new way of living.*

> *"This is about spirit gaining control of the mind or lovingly becoming the overall guide."*

Documented in my journal, the visit noted below was one stay of two where friendly hosts immediately responded to queries as I investigated housing possibilities, revealing the first lesson; those that readily respond often have limited situations and ulterior motives.

My Tucson, AZ friend has no problem sleeping on her small living room couch so there's no need, in her mind, for me to stay in a nearby hotel. I soon arrive at the airport to be escorted to her home, which turns out to be a duplex. Obviously, the ever-changing wheel of involution and evolution continues, for being with someone who three years ago was of very similar mind and now appears near the bottom of a downward spiral is disconcerting at least. It's not so much the negativity and denser energies, which thankfully I'm somewhat able to ignore, but the filth and clutter that permeates this fine woman's space.

It's easy to see where my friend is for I've been there, a dark place where all hope is gone and one spirals into a downward cycle of feeling unworthy of better things. A place where one has massive savings in the form of stocks, bonds, and multiple houses (this one with renters in the back attached unit), a place where we insist on keeping what's left only to lose it. For me, and for my friend, it's all about finally ridding thoughts of limitation. And now, I sure am ready to do that, spending whatever it takes to make me feel comfortable, with no thought of savings for an illusory future.

The week fills with busy things to do as with most typical people who avoid facing their personal issues; my friend plans an almost constant flow of activities. We spend the first day shopping at a local expensive co-op organic food store where I, because of my friend's offer to house me for two-weeks without cost, gladly pay $200 for groceries, including nearly $50 worth of seeds and nuts (that she insists we eat, minced with plain water, for breakfast). Hungry, I treat us to a lovely organic lunch (meeting my ulterior motive to actually eat something pleasurable). The next morning we rise early to meet a planned obligation before food shopping again; this time the second cost of nearly $200 does make me think.

After meeting another morning obligation, we stop at the local farmer's market before volunteering for several hours, assembling newsletters for subscribers at a local lightworker organization, and eating a 'free' vegetarian lunch there when work is complete. Another day finds us traveling to Lemon Mountain for a walk around the lake and lunch, which I gladly pay for, at the new restaurant in a town affected by fires. Thursday night we attend a talk about local Ray Kinema's near-death experience.

Five days later, attempting to function somewhat normally, while being in what I refer to as a "hellhole," previously unthought-of ways to clear dense energies from ones space become very clear; of course, after taking time to get over the shock of what I willingly chose to experience. Finally, after days of less than three hours sleep, I become much more clear about the denser energies in my friend's home, and of course, intuitive senses are verified by her temporary roommate, in the second bedroom, who, she secretly confides, calls in the Hathors for protection until she can spiral out into the light of day by moving elsewhere.

Frankly, I have slept on better daybeds, ones without someone's belongings stuffed under them for lack of storage space. After listening in shocked silence, my friend, to her credit, agrees to drive me to gather necessities that will assist in continuing my stay in her cluttered, filthy bedroom with peeling paint and competing energies, of new age tools such as crystals, forty-year-old non-cotton bedding and neglected antiques. After shopping for new bedding, buying yet more food, and clearing materials from a New Age store, evening finds us sharing dinner and two rounds of hand and foot (a card game) with friends. Later, upon placing a new feather pillow and organic cotton sheets upon the daybed (directly from the wrapper because she has no washer or dryer!), dousing them with frankincense oil, cleansing the area with white sage incense, playing nurturing music on my tiny computer, and lighting a candle for protection and peace, I finally sleep a night of four-plus hours.

Packing light, in one backpack for two weeks of varied weather does have its drawbacks; sometimes we are not equipped or dressed for certain situations. My friend spends time working in the community garden while I search for shady spots to sit away from the smell of animal dung one sunny Tucson morning, all the while intuitively sensing she is there for the free food. The time allows me to begin planning an excursion to Prescott, another place, hours away, which I'm guided to visit.

Mother's Day finds us at a local church service before seeing a great movie, The Artist, at the local theatre. Seeing a well-scripted comedy really helps when continually faced with negative energies so I'm happy to foot the cost! And handling destructive energies, I now confirm, is easier upon grounding by being outside in nature, wearing crystals, taking Epsom salt baths or using a variety of other methods.

Several teachings arose during this first and last stay with my Tucson, AZ friend, the first of which is to always follow intuition, despite what others may believe. Most visits to check out new areas as possibilities and visit friends in the meantime occurred while sleeping at comfy, clutter free hotel rooms. This was one of few exceptions, and yet served to meet soul contracts in a way that could not have been accomplished while sleeping elsewhere. During this two-week AZ stay, I literally refused to move from the car to tour a popular tourist attraction (an astrally dense filled mountain-top town) while on a trip to Sedona; re-connected with an old friend living in Mesa (who helped us avoid an 8-hour accident traffic jam while on the way to visit Prescott); cleared negative energies in multiple places, and opened a portal in the woods of Prescott; assisted my friend's roommate to make the decision to move out of limiting conditions; and assisted my friend in the decision to sell one of her home investments (where clairvoyance clued me into her renters repeated gross Santeria rituals taking place in the windowless cellar). All in all, the knowledge and use of consistent clairvoyance coupled with intuition helped to change perspectives and make each physical experience better.

If one is interested in connecting with one's Higher Self and limiting the influence of denser negative energies it's important to perform several rituals such as assuring your own living space is free of clutter, which draws negative energies just like dust draws more dust.

Of course, for me at least, experience is the best teacher, and it is only after staying with my friend that more ways of eliminating dense energies surfaced. Despite it all, maintaining an attitude of gratitude is vital, especially when one feels nothing to be grateful about!

During this period, daily practices helped to keep my vessel pure, such as spreading the Light within body cells, which usually comes after mentally voicing a prayer of gratitude for unseen assistance and dedicating time, space and everything else to *All That Is* before rising.

Homewood Suites Dense Astral Energies

𝕳ighly discounted suites, one of my daughter's Fortune 500 job perks, make it possible to move from hotel to hotel, a bit too frequently due to rules, while waiting for the perfect place to manifest in North Carolina. As noted in the following journal entry, I decide to try a different hotel chain and am met with the densest of energies experienced to date.

Life challenges me every day since returning to Florida after visiting my friend's cabin in N.C., where I'm currently called to live. The timing of my move remains uncertain. After unexpectedly seeing Samuel, my grandson, at a bus stop, and agreeing to share a late lunch with him, I drive quickly away to check into Homewood Suites.

This will be my first two-week stay in one place since leaving the pristine, two-bedroom suburban sanctuary nearly a month ago. "Why is it so hard to find the entrance?" I think, after passing it twice. Because of the freeway I have to travel two more miles to circle around again!

Living in hotels creates new challenges, one of which is my propensity to pay for things with cash. Paying for hotel stays in dollars instead of tracked credit cards is frowned upon due to government regulations, which warn people to report large cash payments. Nevertheless, I refuse to re-enter the financial system of greed and control and today am fully prepared to pay cash for this stay, plus leave a deposit for incidentals.

Two people greet me after I enter a small, dark building, neither of which ask for identification, or seem surprised when I pull out nearly a thousand dollars to pay for my stay. A sign stating hotel personnel processes refunds above $75 by check sits on the wall to my left, but I disregard it.

"How surprising that they don't require a deposit for incidentals," I think to myself ignoring intuition as the friendly woman behind the counter checks her computer for a suite. Looking around the room, beyond the window towards several small buildings, it's plain to see that this extended-stay hotel is much different from those managed by Rebecca's employer. It sits next to the freeway and isn't as well-kept. This is my first stay in a place where inside corridors do not protect the suite's entrance.

Shoving doubt aside, I quickly immerse myself in another new realm of 3D reality, hauling things up a flight of outside stairs to the new suite, in the middle of a long walkway. A strong sense of deja vu overwhelms me when zipping back downstairs to get the rest of my things. Yes! I recall a dream in which this, or a similar scene, woke me years ago. "How strange to have this dream," I'd thought upon waking next to my husband of sixteen years, "for I'd never be in this type of situation in such a seedy hotel."

Smells of cleaning fluids and cheap air freshener fill the dingy, dark bedroom and small kitchen beyond it. They mask its usual musty smell but I don't know this, yet. I soon head towards a restaurant near Samuel's house after securing my things in the large, mirrored closet that sits in front of a queen-size bed featuring a dark-colored polyester spread.

A small window inside the musty room barely opens when I return to unpack and the other window refuses to open at all. Now, I'm noticing details, as numerous people peek into the room while strolling by. Pictures of butterflies fill the brown, polyester, fiber-filled bedspread, however they fail to comfort me. The carpet and kitchen floor seem dirty, despite smells of detergent, and a small red light, noting a message, flashes on the old telephone. I lift the telephone's receiver appalled to see it caked with filth.

"At least this place has a stove to cook today's shrimp and tomorrow's chicken before they go bad," I think, while reaching for a pan. "That's a blessing." The pan is not clean enough so I wash it again glad to have the tools to do so. People continue to walk by, peeking into the small room's dirty window, while I feel like a fish in a bowl cooking in the kitchen that is clearly visible to them. A busty, French blonde, one of two women in the room next door, stands on the catwalk talking loudly on a cell phone.

Not able to stand the foot traffic and blatant peeks after eating, I close the tattered curtain before filling the bathtub with hot water and Epsom salts. Somehow, it's still surprising to see black mold, which covers the bottom of the empty soap dish. Most people, it seems, don't sit in the tub to take a bath; maybe that's why nobody sees it.

Now ready for sleep, I think it's wonderful to have an unusual spell of cooler weather making it possible to leave the window cracked open. Yet, an unusual amount of foot traffic seems to be on the walkway outside. Is it my imagination, or are the energies much denser now? Am I limiting my intake of breath instead of expanding as I've become accustomed to doing? Why didn't I think to pack the usual sage and what suitcase holds my candle? A very restless night ensues.

Nine o'clock Tuesday morning finds me at the front desk. Shamika, a plump, smiling Jamaican woman from housekeeping, who looks much younger than I, listens intently from several feet away as the desk clerk apologizes for bathroom mold and a filthy telephone. She quickly offers a dishrag and dish soap when I ask for it. Promises to get the requested, more private, second floor corner room with a larger window that opens all the way, in a few days, keeps me happy.

Bleach and cleaning smells soon fill the three small rooms. Housekeeping replaces towels and bedding, including the polyester fiber-filled spread—the new one of which now features a small cigarette burn—but takes the clean dishrag without replacing it. Negative thoughts creep into gray matter to cloud thinking. Was the bedspread that covered me last night dirty from the last guest?

Shamika soon comes to replace the telephone with one she takes right out of the box. Hours later, two men carry out and begin to clean the air conditioning unit, leaving the door wide open. Filled with a sense of privacy invasion, I sit at the kitchen counter, which doubles as a desk, working on a laptop while pretending to be unconcerned. What else can I do? Relief fills me when the short Mexicans finally replace the small wall unit and leave, this time closing the door behind them.

Many working people frequent this hotel, leaving in the morning and returning at night to rest up for another day of labor to pay the rent. I assume the women staying next to me are among them since the room next door remains quiet.

The busty, French blonde again talks on a cell phone as she walks back and forth in front of our rooms at twilight. Foot traffic on the walkway outside my room remains intrusive so now I close the old, dusty drapes to notice tiny holes in them. Still grateful for unexpected cooler weather I hope for more fresh air to fill my space while crawling into bed.

The women in the next room talk loudly, as if fighting, at eleven o'clock in the evening.

"It's my room," I hear one profess.

Sleep remains elusive as one of them then talks with a man on the catwalk after midnight.

Is my imagination working overtime or do surrounding energies again seem much denser? Is that an elongated, gray spirit form hovering near the upper wall in front of me? Glad to have found a candle, I light it before rising to shift through my backpack for the small bottle of frankincense tucked inside on a whim while hurriedly moving from the canal sanctuary.

It takes several tries to light the candle and minutes later the flame is out; despite several attempts, I cannot relight it. Either the matches refuse to spark or the flame goes out when my eyes close. Are the dense energies in this room making it impossible to burn a candle, which to me signifies the presence of God? Filling the room with my own bright light seems the only option as I try to sleep.

Escalating knocks next door soon wake me. The pounding stops after a minute but almost immediately starts again. After another brief respite, someone now bangs upon my door. "Perhaps," I think, remaining safe in the middle of the queen-size bed, "one of the women next door locked her friend out." Intuition prompts me to remain in bed.

Brilliant white light radiates from within while trying to ignore the persistent knocks between 1:10 and 1:35 a.m. There are no hotel personnel at the front desk after eleven o'clock in the evening, and although someone of authority lives in one of the buildings, I don't want to disturb them. Finally desperate, I dial "0" on the new phone. A tired-sounding woman answers after several rings.

"I'll check it out," she announces when I explain my dilemma in a panic.

The knocks abruptly end as soon as we disconnect the call.

"Ah, yes," I think, shrugging while recalling *A Course In Miracles* studies, "ego served its purpose by drawing me into the drama. Light is stronger than denser energies," I affirm, while lying back in bed, expanding the light within to morph further. For the first time, I imagine it reaching 5,000 feet in all directions. Sleep finally comes right before three o'clock in the morning.

Wednesday's light of day brings a bitter reality. Shamika, my earth angel, stands on the stairs three feet away, looking at a clipboard, when I open my door to check out twelve days early at 9:00 AM. She's sorry to hear about the night's events and says hotel personnel noticed that many different men visit the women rooming next to me.

Apparently, they are hookers, but will check out this morning.

One of the women peeks out their suite door, sees us, and quickly closes it. Stating a desire to leave, it's tough not to get into the drama of this dilemma while asking if this type of behavior is normal. Shamika assures me it is not and then quickly reminds me of the sign glanced at days ago when paying for two weeks room rent in advance. Any refund above $75 in cash comes in two weeks by check via mail.

"Oh boy," my growing ego notes, "more dilemmas! Thank goodness I still have a Fort Lauderdale post office box."

Shamika and I continue to talk blocking the stairway, and the hustlers, one by one, have no choice but to pass between us, casting eyes downward sheepishly, after asking for pardons. Continuing to hold the Light with pure thoughts, I bear them no ill will knowing they blessed me with the awareness of yet another way I don't need to live. Silent thoughts of thanks for choosing as a soul to experience such a life makes me happy to know their career, as everyone else's, somehow enriches All That Is.

Shamika assures me there's now a better room available and tomorrow I can move to the more popular and private second-floor corner room steps away. Not wanting to wait for a refund that comes in the mail, I agree to try and stick this stay out. The God Network is working. Calls from my friend in

Arizona, my friend in N.C., and Phillip, thirty minutes away, fill the next hour, while Shamika makes sure the next room is up to her standards. Phillip seems intent on seeing me as soon as possible so I know he's tuned into my situation. I agree to meet him for lunch after moving to the new room.

She's on her way to get me, my earth angel soon phones to say. A lower, corner room in the building farthest from highway traffic is ready to meet my approval. Minutes later I stare to my left, beyond a hedge, to see a small man-made lake yards from the room. But the hotel garbage bin sits yards ahead of the only window, which faces a parking lot. Cleaning smells again mask the musty smelling air conditioning unit. Shamika has clearly done her best to make this room as attractive as possible. But there's no way she can move beyond the limitations of this hotel.

As I waver, she assures me that this wing consists of "real" working people who are gone for most of the day so it's quiet here. I note my sensitivity to smell, but agree to try and stick it out for the night until the more private room is ready. In the back of my mind, as I open the window as far as it will go to try and clear the room, I'm not sure that I want to move back to the building just left. Shamika cautions me against keeping the window open during the night and notes the pin to stop it from opening fully is missing. Since she'll be in the area for another hour, she agrees to close it for me before leaving so I can meet

Phillip for lunch. She'll also replace the missing pin.

Passing other rooms after unloading the cooler from my car gives me a bird's eye view as housekeeping cleans. Open doors reveal carpets littered with beer cans, pizza boxes, and other debris. Several mattresses and an old couch sit near the garbage bin. I'm not sure if they're new or old for they're covered in plastic. Resigned to stay, I leave to meet Phillip for a late breakfast at one o'clock after placing perishables in the clean refrigerator.

Phillip soon assures me this experience is indeed meeting a greater purpose and I'm to document the journey for those on the same path. He then reminds me not to seek outside my Self for we must trust our intuition fully; we are indeed humanities proxies. After a lovely lunch, I leave to stock up on more fresh, organic food, happy to have connected with such a like-mind.

Golden orbs appear in the cloudless, blue sky, as I sit on the lawn outside the new room after storing groceries. They remind me that all is indeed well. They, whoever "they" are, watch over me and it is indeed delightful to again see them, miniscule points of brilliant white light, with this body's physical eyes.

Before sleep, I recall two extended stay hotels near my storage unit, check availability, and then recheck Marriott. Yes, despite hotel rules, and a strong desire to remain out of the system of greed and manipulation, I'll move on for the energy here is not to my liking. The comforting thought allows me to sleep as the candle burns brightly.

By eleven o'clock the next morning, I'm settled into a safe suburban Marriott sanctuary at three times the cost of Homewood Suites. The only thing that matters is that I'm finally in an area with much lighter energies.

Being able to tap into astral energies has both drawbacks and blessings! And now, years later, I'm aware of the necessity for this eye-opening experience.

Adjusting To Higher Frequencies

Dizziness continues to overwhelm me upon waking as the room spins while trying to sit up. How difficult it is to grip walls and ever so slowly get to the bathroom! I'm very hot and recall waking many times with a runny nose, watery eyes, and bits and pieces of other realm adventures. In one, I taught people about subatomic particles (as if I even know what they are in this life!)—as noted in my Microsoft Bookshelf '95 Dictionary: "Any of various units of matter below the size of an atom, including the elementary particles and hadrons."

In another part of the dream, I told everyone that EVERYTHING is illusion so it doesn't matter, even if you are in the astral world. EVERYTHING is an illusion. EVERYTHING is a dream. This is NOT who we are. We are Love! We are Light! We are formless, not human.

Complete exhaustion overwhelms me as it rains periodically while heavy construction, including drilling, hammering, etc., continues outside the building in which I now reside. I cannot get out of bed to rise for the day until one o'clock in the afternoon. Wow, what a ride!

This then is what it's like as we first incorporate still higher frequencies until finally coalescing them to the point where no dizziness occurs. In the meantime, along with other things, we can employ the 'crazy eyes' method, jotting both open eyes quickly up and down, back and forth, and around.

Often, during these times of heightened frequencies, messages like the one below flow easily through me.

"You are moving into another dimension of your time and space. We are the Lemurian Council of Twelve and we are here to assist you. The dizziness you feel is a difference between the frequencies in dimensions. The frequencies in magnetics of your earth are changing more rapidly than ever before. It is important that you continue to ground yourself using Mother Earth herself. You must do this daily. You must walk on your Mother Earth to more fully coalesce with the frequency in magnetics within her. This is your soul's charge. If you do not wish to follow this soul plan you do not need to do so but cementing these energies, more fully coalescing with the frequencies and magnetics of your Mother Earth, will assist you to do so.

"We are with all those now ready to make this switch in frequency. As your earth frequency and magnetics continue to change, many shall experience what is commonly referred to as vertigo. To lessen the trauma of this experience it is necessary to perform this grounding daily. We are with you as you move though this process. We are the Lemurian Council of Twelve and we wish you to know you are never alone. This process is one that has been moved through in previous times upon your earth. This is the last coalescing of energies, of frequencies and magnetics your earth shall

experience. This shall take an age as you define it of two-thousand years. This age has begun on your 12/21/2012. Although you may seem human, you are not. You are a soul using a human form to experience through the experience of time.

"We are with you now as you move through this process and you may call upon us to assist you at any time. We are the Lemurian Council of Twelve."

Consciously living as a multidimensional HU-man makes it vital to monitor what we choose to put into our brain daily because our brain processes everything seen, heard, or experienced during sleep. Pay special attention to what is read, watched or experienced because it is our brain, our mind, which keeps us locked into physical bodies, this illusion of earth life. It pays greatly to concentrate on things such as *The Science Of Mind, A Course In Miracles* and other esoteric/metaphysical literature. One can start by making sure that daily activities do not keep one in limitation or limit one in any way, and if they physically seem to do so one can change their perspective. There's always a multitude of perspectives to choose from, readily available to raise our frequency.

Yonder Classes

This excerpt from *Book of One :-) Volume 5* documents an instance of tapping into other aspects of the HU-man multidimensional self making it possible to subsequently bring those experiences into the current physical experience.

In the midst of a government shut-in, some people are now using video conferencing software, which I'm leery of using due to my seeming karmic experience as using technology to gather private data and control the masses during the Atlantean Age. Having researched owner data for the most popular software used, it only confirms my choice to avoid this type of technology to conduct bi-monthly classes. Why do people not question the availability of so-called free software that allows others to invade their privacy and access their computer files? Today, upon waking, I am well aware of avoiding the use of this intrusive technology by inviting certain previous class attendees to a class conducted on the ethereal realm of consciousness.

During class, I led the small group through a mind experiment where we check three prominent bodies: the physical, astral and ethereal. Class excerpts are below.

Physical Body: *Be aware of aches and pains as clues to the body's changing DNA, for we are once again taking on the 12 strands of DNA used to experience earth life aeons ago. This does cause aches and pains (imagine, if you will, living in a body that is dying but at the same time rejuvenating). Assuring that the body is flushed with good water (spring water, bottled at the source is best as it contains the live energy of Mother Gaia) assists the process of clearing old cells.*

Astral Body *(auric field before the etheric and dense body): Envision your astral body and check for tears or weak areas, which are evident upon emotional reactions. Clear all judgment; recognize the human's true state as souls here to experience and express and remain in a state of neutrality to avoid negative attractions.*

Ethereal Body *(auric field between the dense physical form and astral field): Continue to fill your ethereal body with Love and Light; remain in your own field of consciousness and be continuously open to guidance from your own Higher Self.*

Class concluded with a round of three vocalized OMs.

Zoning Into 5D Consciousness

The following excerpt from *Book of One :-) Volume 5* reveals how one with a high vibrational rate, tapped into their Higher Self, can live in an individual 5D condition of consciousness while physically in a 3D world.

Life continues to amaze and delight as I follow what many refer to as higher intuition. Today, thoughts of leaving behind the fear mongering state, now held locally by many home-imprisoned people due to mandates, to take money out of the bank repeated, while under what also appears as world-wide government restrictions. I finally gave in and left the apartment. Wondering if my favored parking spot would be open upon my return, a constant serenade of singing birds graced me to and from the six-block ride to my bank. Unmasked young families strolled down streets as smiling people riding bicycles rode by at a leisurely pace. It seemed like a much different world than that seen from my windows, where masked seniors shuffle about only when absolutely necessary to leave their much watched television filled with propaganda.

I soon returned more filled with love and joy than ever before in my short human history of nearly seventy years. As usual, upon finding my parking spot open (a small miracle here where there are no assigned spots and everyone prefers to park in the small lot outside my second-story window), and walking towards the front door of my building, the thought of walking to the water's edge controlled both legs. What a lovely day to once again sit overlooking the very wide expanse of water to bridge both lower and upper worlds, bringing in and grounding the Light of One! Upon finishing this joy-filled task I again headed home, amazed while watching violet light stream from the sun to cleanse earth.

Before reaching the glass door of my building, intuition guided me to stop at the mailboxes, for only the third time in the three years lived in this 300 apartment senior community. You see, living within a fairly constant state of 5D has led to many diversions from 3D reality, which I usually find ways to avoid. The need to waft through piles of daily advertisements and unnecessary mail, welcomed by bored seniors who cherish daily mailbox gathering time, is one of those elements that I have found a way to prevent—by paying for and forwarding all mail to a post office box miles away. Oddly, the mail system will not forward junk mail nor does the post office fill boxes with junk mail! Imagine my surprise upon opening the unused mail box steps from my door to find mail addressed to neighbors and a key to obtain larger mail. Now, imagine the surprise of someone who waited weeks to find out what happened to the love-filled gift sent from an adult child living in New York to their ailing parent. I was fortunate enough to deliver that unopened gift after removing it from its misdirected perch.

One may wonder no more about what it is like to live in a 5D state of consciousness for this is what it's all about, listening to, and following subtle guidance from one's Higher Self; and when we do miracles become ordinary occurrences!

Opening Portals

℘ortals to other dimensions with higher frequencies are easily accessible, while on the cusp of sleep; but continuing into them, our frequency must change. This is the reason for the increasing energies coming to earth now. As earth changes, so too do our body's magnetics, allowing us to connect to higher dimensions. These dimensions are more in tune to the crystalline structure our physical body now morphs into.

Looking back, it's difficult to pinpoint the first time I was intuitively guided to open or stand in a portal, but if I had to name a time and place it would be during vacation, on a 2007 birthday cruise in the Caribbean with my daughter. As she walked ahead towards the designated barbeque lunch spot I felt drawn to stop and raise closed eyes and outstretched arms to the sky, while basking in the brilliant sun. It seemed as if I was being guided as to what to do, when to slowly lower both arms in a circular motion, before clasping them as if in prayer with a slight bow. And now, many years later, it's clear; that was when I began to bring in higher frequencies, to start yet another exciting sequence of experience and expression, never experienced or expressed before. Many portals have since beckoned me, experiences of some which are noted below.

North Carolina Portal

Sometimes experiences are not at all what we expect or envision and my eight-month North Carolina stay certainly proved this to me. One of the unknown reasons for my stay in two cabins, moving from an unneeded much larger one to a smaller space across the street, as noted in the journal entry below, was to welcome in year-end energies of 2012.

Life here in the woods of North Carolina is quite different from the hustle and bustle of cities like Fort Lauderdale. Wild turkeys roam the area and sirens very, very, very rarely mar the peace and exquisite higher vibrating energies. Noisy airplanes rarely glide through the air. Things to keep people in lower vibrational states of living, such as wi-fi, seem much harder to get, and thankfully, airwaves seem empty of the constant onslaught of cell phones, satellite dishes, and other invisible detriments to peaceful living.

A chorus of crickets draws me outside to "Be one with It." Low-lying clouds seem to fill dusk surrounding the cabin as I raise my arms to connect with the grid of Light. It's warmer now than hours ago and clear that rain sits nearby as I share the Light, spreading it outward from this private land, to city, to state, the globe and beyond. Wind builds as I move around the porch continuing the task while hearing whispers of tourists in a nearby cabin. How wonderful to once again feel one with It!

Another calling completes during the following month.

Continually radiating the heart's energy and raising this body's vibration and Light quotient is now habitual. Many people pray, meditate, and otherwise lift humanity in their own way, either as part of a group or physically alone, on the auspicious day of 12-21-12. The thought of morphing to Light entertained me for many months, but now I don't expect much personally, yet wish for the highest aspect of humanity to break forth though the ethers of space and time, into a more life-affirming frequency. As we remain in physical form, it seems high time to do so with a passion for life, in joy, abundance, peace, wholeness and full of all the good there is. Well aware that Higher Self now leads all who wish to move forward into greater states of loving awareness, I let go of the past as greater frequencies fill and surround earth.

Strong winds wake me shortly after eleven o'clock in the morning to see sun streaming in from a far window. The anticipated birds are not chirping but I rise refreshed and ready to begin the first day of this New Earth; this, I remind myself, is why I've come. Although winds remain strong, I must venture outside. Ecstasy fills me while eating fresh oatmeal with flaxseeds, raisins, and butter. My hands warm holding the pan as pine trees sway in unison and unrelenting wind blasts move through the woods. Focusing attention on finishing the meal, I try to ignore cooler temperatures and finish eating quickly. After waiting many, many eons, living many, many, earth lives, traveling other realms, and being pushed ahead of many other souls, I know there's a task to complete.

Scant minutes before 12:21 PM, I stand facing the sun, in the middle of the front 'yard' (such that it is, a half-acre of mainly dirt), with arms held up to the sky to do my part. I anchor the New Earth for humanity, with tears of joy streaming down rosy cheeks, while wind continues to blast through the area. Several minutes later, after voicing thanks to those who stepped aside to allow me this pleasure, I sit upon my favorite large rock, touching a stone on either side, while again anchoring the energies through my body to the earth.

Yet, knowing that ultimately all here is illusion, merely an experience and expression of unique frequencies, I did not plan the day or have any expectations. Still, I know, this is exactly what I came here to do. What a blessing it is to be one, of many souls, who came specifically for this day!

Ego's limiting ways are forgotten as, once again, the daily need for fresh salad pushes me forward, down mountains and around bending roads. Although I had no expectations as to how this day would unfold, I did plan to remain in my physical sanctuary of one. But as tall pines continue to sway in today's strong winds I too am learning to move with the flow, pushing further through old beliefs and thought patterns.

Cardinal Grand Cross Alignment Portal

What a grand experience it will be to stand in a portal welcoming the energies of the Cardinal Grand Cross alignment! Mars, Jupiter, Uranus, Pluto and the Sun begin to exactly align as few unawakened people play on the beach amid cloudy, dark skies. Of course, intuition drives me outside more than thirty minutes before 8:01 PM and, surprisingly, the portal is in perfect alignment with the house so all I need do is walk across the street.

A bright beacon of red-golden light stands out, about seventy feet away, toward the east in the water, like a sore thumb, as I stare in awe. No one else seems to notice. It takes me several minutes to realize it's the sun hitting one of several buoys, dead on. Not believing there's no need to walk the beach to find the portal, I think, "It can't be this easy," and begin moving in the usual north direction. Two beautiful, small, white birds take turns dive-bombing in the water, as if to draw my attention, and since I've never seen such striking, slim looking birds; it's clear, these gatekeepers are showing me the portal.

"This is the place," they seem to say.

Yet, not trusting my initial intuition, or the flying creatures, I walk the usual route to make sure the portal isn't farther away. Almost ten minutes before 8:01 PM, I return to the first site to find a tall, muscular young man standing steps away, further down the beach to my right, where he remains, scooping water onto his arms as I welcome the energies in my own guided way.

At one point, probably exactly when the planets align, I seem to leave my physical body for what seems as a split second. An emergency vehicle passing on the highway brings me back; yet, a sense of changing energies remain, despite the 3D distraction, and I smile with the thought of now moving into greater service for humanity, fully supported by unseen realms.

Riding Out Hurricane Irma

*I*n addition to a small portable power system to recharge laptops, cell phone, and small appliances, two fully charged laptop batteries, canned foods, a stock of spring water, toilet paper, and Kleenex now sits in closets as Florida's hurricane season unfolds. Having survived several hurricanes, most notably Wilma (as described in *The End Of My Soap Opera Life: A Change In Perception*), there's no need to take a chance on experiencing group possibilities due to lower frequency ways of living during the beginning storm on Friday, September 9, 2017. Intuition continues to assure my safety after moving further from the beach into the back portion of a duplex.

It's business as usual, for me, until Hurricane Irma's winds finally knock out the neighborhood's power on Saturday around 9:30 PM. Before the core reaches us in the expected two-plus hours, I take the time to silently ask.

"Is there anything I need do now?"

"We are with you now as these winds of time shift and change the very nature of your world and neighborhoods. We are keeping close watch on those ready to report and listen. It is time to report the trends of the New Earth and this will be done by those moving through these vast changes. You all came for this final call and it is with the greatest of pleasure that we watch while you bravely weather the trials and tribulations on your earth.

"For you personally, you have taken the necessary steps and all is in readiness for your next phase. Continue to listen to that still, small voice within to guide you in the hours ahead; it is all we have to relate at this time. You are safe in your neighborhood hammock, nestled in a place that is secure from stronger destructive winds and rain. Choose your experience by your willingness to receive."

Obviously, I now consciously agree to accept all offers and gifts.

Strong winds blow through cracks between jalousie windows as I consider options after hours of reading, while in the Lazy Boy, which I've placed in the middle of the living room. Is it safe to move to the bedroom? Tree branches periodically fall upon the roof as human thoughts persistently surface. Are the three trees on this property able to withstand Irma's winds?

Radiating heart energy seems like the only thing to do, so I lie spread-eagle upon the bed feeling waves of unremitting energy course through the mind-body. Fear wafts through darkness as the wind train becomes stronger but I replace it with the truth of "I AM," rising only to satisfy thirst and use the toilet. Radiating heart energy becomes easy to do as the wind train blasts through trees. Fleeting seconds of fear dissipate while repeating "I AM," all the while radiating heart energy out into the atmosphere. "Only good will come of this," I continue to repeat. Sleep finally claims me shortly before 3:00 AM.

Spirit continues to flow though lit candles while I rise to peek out the now dirty slat windows to see a debris-filled back yard, three shade trees down, and surprisingly, an intact aluminum storage unit still without a front door. Irma finishes ripping through our area of Fort Lauderdale, Florida on Sunday afternoon. Although two small trees in the backyard uprooted, and one fell onto the roof of the bedroom (where I slept knowing of the possibility but allowing myself to move with the flow), there's no damage to the house itself.

And now after five days without power, but the ability to drive nearby for necessities, and Phillip's assistance in recharging the portable power system, I silently hear this is another time to let go, to trust that needs will continue to be taken care of. So far, aside from hearing neighborhood generator noise (new since last night), and the consistent heat of our Florida weather, it's not as bad as it could have been. Area store shelves pretty much remain bare but it seems that other neighborhoods, ten or so miles away, which got power restored days ago, are getting deliveries, but food is quickly snapped up as soon as it gets on the shelves. Thank goodness for intuition allowing a stock of usual foods!

Some house power returns after day six, the refrigerator works and so does one light switch in the bath, and oddly the washer and dryer. I quickly assume that Florida Power and Light (FPL) cut the power as they continue work in the neighborhood; houses across the street and others still have no power. Yet, I'm guided to be diligent and phone FPL. The lady with a cold, who I'm divinely guided to after minutes of dealing with an annoying computer, says the house is not getting enough voltage. So even if she does not know what that means it confirms my belief. Hopefully, FPL will increase the voltage to where it should be upon dealing with damaged wires from downed trees. Surely, only good will come of these experiences, I think, while silently blessing the FPL representative with good health before ending our conversation.

Yes, there is always another reason for events, recognized when one taps into varied states of perception. This is clearly part of my 'Lightworker Training,' I know upon hearing: "Just continue to BE and breathe. You are living by faith now, allowing the Universe to guide. Go out and create in the New World for the foundation is firmly solid."

Changing Perspective Through
Multidimensional Living

𝔙ibrant energy filled the room as I took my seat in the meeting room among strangers that seemed familiar, some more than most. It didn't take much time to identify past life experiences with numerous members of the small group. Yes, the sense of knowing them in past lives persisted throughout our few days together, during sessions, shared meals, and outside activities. A knowing of our past connection with the Theosophical Society came over me as my new friend and I walked to the nearby dollar store, but for some people in our group there was just a hint of familiarity, and not knowing perspectives I remained silent as to information received through my sixth sense.

One, always smiling, tall and vibrant young man stood out among the rest. Nevertheless, despite what appeared a shared desire to engage in private conversation, daily events, separate building accommodations, and my own lack of energy stemmed the flow. As we all said our goodbyes after the last session a strong wave of loss surprised me over not being able to connect with the vibrant young man whose kindly mannerisms reminded me of my grandson. But fate would see that we connected privately in what to me seemed a miraculous way.

The fleeting thought of a long, lonely ride back to the airport permeated my mind while waiting for the small, black limo; but it was interrupted by the sound of someone approaching, so what could have been a downward spiral was immediately curtailed. There he soon stood before me with his million-dollar smile and a back pack on his strong back just as our driver arrived.

We spent our time sharing revelations and ideas as familiarity permeated the air, causing, at least for me, a great dislike at the thought of parting, perhaps never to be seen again. But since his flight was later than mine, he promised to find me before boarding; after all, he had plenty of time before his flight left for Ohio.

"What a feat that would be," I thought to myself, as he left to check in at another terminal in the vast Chicago airport.

All hopes of seeing him again left when my boarding gate changed to a different terminal as well. But just as I took my seat after rushing through terminals to find the correct one, his smiling, exuberant face and long stride filled my vision, and in my mind he seemed to say, "I told you I'd find you."

Our private talk was meant to be and when it was done we hugged with tear-filled eyes. Yes, my Lemurian son reminded me there have been many lives and many children, and although in this life it seems that I've lost a son our uplifting meeting left me with a great sense of gaining one.

Multidimensional Living While Physically In 4D

While humanity made the shift to 4D—the emotional realm of consciousness—that brings ever-changing and increasing waves of drama to offer opportunities for greater evolution, a much smaller group of humanity paved the way to even greater realms of Consciousness. And yet, drama still creeps in for those of us living a multidimensional life, continuing to hold thoughts of unity within this space, and walking our talk.

A clear understanding of frequency and vibration is necessary while living a multidimensional life and it's vital to consistently recall what some refer to as the Law of Attraction, for like frequencies attract. Keeping the body's vibrational rate as high as possible helps to avoid many 'normal' living circumstances, which only serve to lower one's frequency. For me, among other methods, that means changing my way of living to limit harmful frequencies (by avoiding crowds of unawakened people or using a quiet vacuum cleaner, etc.); avoiding unnecessary loss of time and energy (by paying for a Post Office (P.O.) Box to avoid daily junk mail and mail misdirection, etc.); and keeping a low-profile. But clearly, there are times when we must interact with someone, and sometimes those interactions not only take us out of our comfort zones but have the potential to lower the body's frequency.

Periodic bouts of drama seem unescapable for me while associating with those holding on to out-dated habits and ways of living. The following account details how one living a multidimensional life can move through these periodic bouts of what seems as unescapable drama by using a few vital tools enlisted by multidimensional beings. These include, but are not limited to: listening to intuition; paying attention to subtle physical clues; and being conscious of reactions, emotions, thoughts, words and deeds and consistently changing them to match higher states of Consciousness. As you read through this account find the clues that assisted me while moving through the circumstance.

A choice to increasingly serve humanity above striving to make ends meet, by working 16-hour days for other people, fueled my current housing decision in 2017. With that choice came rules, regulations, and an entirely different way of living, but, of course, the Universe thoroughly prepared me for those changes starting from April 1, 2012 (all joking aside). So here I am in the midst of massive global change during 2021, minding my own business and keeping a low profile, when yet again, my only friend who has supported my decision in a multitude of ways and has the habit of moving me out of my comfort zone, strikes again.

Over the course of several years, I have consistently reminded my friend that any mail is to be sent to the P.O. Box I've held since the late 1990's. Numerous conversations where the reasons were clearly stated, in my mind, occurred and following my own intuition I held firm to the knowledge that a P.O. Box was the best way for me to receive mail. But of course, the day came, as always, on December 21st, when my friend thought it best to follow his own habits and phoned to let me know a late birthday card was on the way to my community apartment's mail system. I affirmed, having been blessed with the previous tenant's request to forward her mail to her new address that this delivery would not bring on an increase of junk mail. I only check the apartment mail box when intuition alerts me to do so (refer to *Zoning Into 5D Consciousness* on page 177), sometimes not for a year at a time. Upon checking my mail box, finding a Christmas card but no birthday card, I phoned my friend with the news, again to be met with his doubts of my receiving the birthday card. Now, I suspected he sent more than a card and affirmed it would arrive.

My friend phoned two days later to ask if the birthday card arrived and again voiced concern that it might get lost. I knew then he'd sent more than a card and again affirmed that the correspondence would arrive. Knowing his beliefs, that cash gifts should not be sent via mail, despite my relayed previous experiences of sending thousands of dollars via regular mail to publishers, and receiving bits of cash throughout the years, I checked the box again, even knowing it was not there. The next day upon phoning him to report, he again voiced concern filled again with what I consider outdated thoughts, so I again affirmed that the card would arrive.

On Christmas Eve, guided to look out my window, I saw a man with a tiny dog near the mail boxes but again sensed the card was not in my mailbox. Christmas Day found me strolling around the community and while passing by the bevy of mail boxes near my apartment I looked down at the ground to see what appeared as shiny sparkles, what seemed as the same pretty but troublesome tiny confetti sparkles my friend usually encloses with cards. When I passed the next bevy of mailboxes there were several pieces of misdirected mail tucked into crevices near the intended recipients mail box.

Bright and early, on Monday, December 27th, shortly after the apartment complex office opened, the administrator phoned to alert me that a resident held my misdirected mail, which had been opened. I was to see the resident who held my mail to get an explanation along with the mail. Of course, after having a rough night of dealing with increased geomagnetic activity, unable to sleep until dawn, I was exhausted, but nevertheless, dressed to retrieve the card. I knew this man wanted to meet me in person, for having read my mail he was now curious.

He stood at his door with a tiny dog as I approached and soon apologized for not returning my mail sooner. Since he "didn't like" a tenant in my building he would not enter it and thought it best to alert the office and have them phone me. The saga of the misdirected birthday card unfolded, first from what seemed an honest man who found it in his mail box and placed it in a crevice near my mail box, to the man now telling the story who demanded it from a strange woman who tore the envelope open and voiced an inaudible yes coupled with a joyful downward fist, as if in acknowledgement of a found treasure. Since he had spoken with the man who found the misdirected mail in his box and had seen me looking down from my window, he knew something was amiss. Apparently, the non-resident stranger was in the habit of stealing mail and having been the Community Director at one time this man wanted to be sure I got what I was "supposed to get." With another apology for reading the card, which was unavoidable since it was a single cardboard sheet instead of the usual folded card, he handed me the large manila envelope that the office had put it into. Thus ends the tale of competing energies.

Remember, first, reactions, emotions, words, thoughts and deeds build the world and the time lapse between these and manifestation lessens daily; second, the higher frequencies will always override outdated lower frequencies.

Cusp Of Sleep Channel: Law Of One
Higher Self Message

As monads we experience a wide variety of expressions, all of which are retained by our Spiritual Soul (yet another, although lower frequency aspect of expressions that shall eventually be dissipated). The following is a journal entry of connecting to my Spiritual Soul.

More words come as I lie in bed on the cusp of sleep yet again.

"I shall read to you from the Law of One. Are you ready to transcribe?"

"Yes," I reply, reaching for the bedside recorder.

*"The Law of One is simply this: **There is One, there is no other.** Treat all as you would yourself. When you treat yourself as gold, as perfection, as Truth, as the one most treasured above all else, you know then that this is the way to treat others. But first, the masses must see themselves as that gold, that perfection. This is happening now in your world. Once all treat each other using the Law of One, the Eden you all seem to think you left so long ago returns.*

"The Law of One most simply put is this: The BEingness within you returns to the Oneness of all things. The BEingness within you is the Law of One. The Law surrounds you, even

now, as many strive to avoid the mass confusion surrounding them. *The Law of One shines ever so brightly within the hearts of those even as they strive to stay part of the disappearing reality in which they seem to live. The Law of One unfolds quickly now upon your earth.*

"*Know that all things change. The Law of One is everlasting. Live the Law of One and you shall see how the world changes quickly before you. There is no other law to concentrate on at this time. The Law of One supersedes all laws. You know this in your heart, in your very soul. The Law of One supersedes all laws. Treat others as you would yourself, most treasured, knowing the Law of One abides in all realities waiting to be recognized, fully and completely, by all who sense the BEingness of their Being.*

"*Go forth and spread the Law of One. Perfection lies within all waiting to unfold in a streaming moment of glory. This is the rapture many speak of. The Law of One returns to the homeless of all Beings having never really left at all.*"

Cusp Of Sleep Channel:
Multidimensional Living

As these energetic waves of consciousness continue to move into the earth, I clearly recognize the truth we were told so many years ago; energy affects people in different ways. Some people deal with this energy by being angry. We can help those and others around us by spreading love and light if we are ever in the midst of anger. For instance, in the senior community where I live sometimes people are very angry and yelling when geomagnetic energies are high. When this occurs (and other times as well) I radiate Love from my heart's core to fill individuals and the area. This not only helps the body of which my soul experiences physicality, but assists the community as well, for remember everything is energy radiating out into space; so when you focus on your heart's core and radiate that loving energy out into the world, you help not only your own body but the bodies of all those around you. And that radiation of loving energy, as a ripple upon calm waters, continues to spread throughout the earth and beyond it. This is a very practical tip one can employ during times when anger within people seems to rise.

Remember, we can choose to be in the chaos, or not. The end result of chaos is always nirvana, but we must first move through that chaos. We can choose to match and feed chaotic energies or we can choose to neutralize them and nurture harmonious thoughts by radiating loving energy out into the world.

As humanity continues to spiral up in consciousness those not yet ready to leave the matrix of experience and expression in earth time and space shall leave the consciousness of those willing to maintain a steady progress towards greater Light. The channel below confirms this body's knowing.

"We are the White Winged Consciousness of Nine and we are here to report to those who wish to awaken from the dream within the dream. The erasure of your (3D) world moves forward as all on planet earth sense the energies of Oneness. The Oneness within these energies secures a more steady spot in placement upon the earth of Oneness (the New 5D Earth). The reality of many people now dissipates into this Oneness while those not yet awakened become mired in the disappointment of separation. This separation tears apart all those wishing to remain within it; by this tearing apart, we mean the separation keeps those at a distance from others within the Oneness.

"There is no blending of the two when it comes to families, to friends, to those that know the truth. You many wish to interact with one another but the circumstances within each life will not coalesce. The interactions between those in separation and those in Oneness will not be as strong as days past. The interactions to those in separation from those in Oneness will be, for the most part,

planned events, events where plans have been set aside to address those in separation. And yet, this addressing will not occur under the best of circumstances, for those in separation will be hindered with many issues. These issues will keep them in the separation in which their soul seeks to dwell.

"Those within the separation are living within their soul plan and shall remain in separation throughout this lifetime. We ask that those in the state of Oneness know that each soul has made a choice. Each soul's balance will be achieved eventually, if not in this lifetime in yet another. And we ask you to have patience with those still mired in the throes of separation for the Oneness of which all seek lies within.

"We are the White Winged Consciousness of Nine and we are here to report on the steadiness of the Oneness which fills planet earth."

This was, I now admit, a bit difficult to channel while on the cusp of waking from deep sleep consciousness, for noise related to a thunderstorm and construction in the building began. Nevertheless, I persisted, remembering that we must successfully deal with distractions, while continuing to perform higher vibrational tasks. And now, as the so-called pandemic (otherwise known as plandemic) unfolds, the meaning of this message is clearly understood.

Doubts of living as a multidimensional being dissipate, and as guidance continues it is obvious; this state of BEing, a free-flowing movement into unknown territory, is the only way to continue playing the game of earth life.

About The Author

Sharon Ann Meyer (aka SAM), author of the "Lightworker's Log Book Series," is a minister (ordained by Sanctuary of the Beloved Church Priesthood and Order of Melchizedek), channel of higher realms, metaphysical teacher, founder of SAM, I AM PROductions — SamIAMproductions.com — and administrator of the popular Internet resource, Lightworker's Log.

Spreading Spirit's message of Oneness throughout the globe, SAM is a wayshower helping humanity to learn the truth of BEing so humanity can unfold from within and return all unique figments back to *All That Is*.

The Lightworker's Log Book Series

- *Book One: Death of the Sun*
- *Book Two: A Change in Perception*
- *Lightworker's Log :-) Transformation*
- *Manifesting: Lightworker's Log*
- *Prayer Treatments: Lightworker's Log*
- *Adventures in Greece and Turkey*
- *Earth Angels*
- *Return to Light: John of God Helps*
- *Bits of Wisdom*

- *Book of One :-) Volume 1*
- *Book of One :-) Volume 2*
- *Book of One :-) Volume 3*
- *Book of One :-) Volume 4*
- *Book of One :-) Volume 5*
- *After Death, Communications…WOW!*
- *Multidimensional Living: Moving Beyond Astral Adventures*